Wallraf-Richartz Museum   Cologne

Rainer Budde and senior curators

Wallraf-Richartz Museum   Cologne

SCALA BOOKS

First published in 1993 by
Scala Publications Ltd
3 Greek Street
London W1V 6NX

and C. H. Beck'sche Verlagsbuchhandlung
Wilhelmstrasse 9
8000 Munich

ISBN 1 870248 76 7

Designed by Alan Bartram
Translated by Elizabeth Thussu
English text edited by Paul Holberton
Produced by Scala Publications
Filmset by August Filmsetting, St Helens, England
Printed and bound in Italy by Graphicom, Vicenza

Contents

The history of the Wallraf-Richartz Museum and its collections

Ferdinand Franz Wallraf, by the terms of whose will the Wallraf-Richartz Museum of Cologne was established on his death on 18 March 1824, was born in Cologne on 27 July 1748. He studied philosophy, theology and medicine at the city's Old University and in 1772 he was ordained priest. In December 1793 he was elected Rector of the University, an office he occupied until the arrival of the French in 1797. In the following years he taught history and aesthetics at the Ecole Centrale, which had replaced the university after the Napoleonic authorities had closed it down.

Wallraf had started collecting early in his career, at first objects for teaching and observation, but then, increasingly, works of art. The process of secularization brought into the open and on to the market countless works of art which he rescued for his collection. His bequest to the city of Cologne was immense, comprising 1,616 paintings, 521 manuscripts, 466 documents, 3,089 seals, 13,248 books, 38,254 engravings, 3,165 woodcuts, 3,875 drawings, 124 classical sculptures, numerous cut stones, coins, fossils, minerals, stained glass, weapons, and much more.

Wallraf had on many occasions let the authorities know of his intention to leave his collection to his native city on his death, with the aim of making it accessible to the public. In 1815, during his lifetime, part of the collection was temporarily housed on the top floor of the former Jesuit College, following the intervention of the President of the Prussian Government, Graf Solms-Lauterbach, as Wallraf's apartment in the Cathedral buildings had long become too full. As a result an inventory could be begun, the 'Wallraf Inventory' made in 1817-18 by Matthias Joseph de Noël (1782-1849). On 1 September 1819 the city council finally agreed to accept the collection with an annuity for its upkeep of 4,000 thalers.

In his last will and testament of 9 May 1819, paragraph 9, Wallraf made the following stipulation: 'I hereby bequeath my entire estate, of whatever it may consist on my death, to my birthplace, the city and community of Cologne, on the express and absolute condition that my collection of art, minerals, paintings, engravings, and books remains with the city and community for all time in the service of Art and Science, that they should maintain it and in no circumstance allow it to be sold, disposed of or removed, or the collection will be withdrawn.' He added further that a museum commission should be set up under the auspices of the city Oberburgermeister to administer the collection, with the task of appointing a 'proper curator for the whole collection with a commensurate salary'.

After Wallraf's death space for the collection was found in the rooms of the Kölner Hof at no. 7 Trankgasse, the former residence of the Archbishop of Cologne. As early as 8 July 1827 a few rooms arranged by de Noël were opened to the public. On 7 May 1828 the city council appointed de Noël to be the first curator of the Wallraf collection, which was now generally known as the 'Wallrafianum'.

The dark and cramped rooms of the Kölner Hof provided inadequate accommodation for the Wallrafianum, especially since the building, dating from the eighteenth century, was in a very sorry state. Even while de Noël held his post – in 1842 he resigned in despair – works of art had been sold off by the council. In 1833, 294 paintings from the collection had been sold for 550 thalers to the art dealer Edward Solly. (The scandalous practice of selling off works of art, from which the Wallraf-Richartz Museum suffered

Egidius Mengelberg, *Ferdinand Franz Wallraf*, 1824

greatly, reached its height during the 1920s and 1930s.) In November 1843, the city council agreed the appointment of the painter Johann Anton Ramboux from Trier (1790-1866) as de Noël's successor.

Much needed provision for the Museum had long been under discussion. In 1828 Jakob Hittorff, a pupil of Wallraf, had sent plans for a new museum from Paris. But they could not be carried out for lack of funds. As soon as he took office, Ramboux complained in various memoranda about the inadequacy of the accommodation for the works of art. On 3 August 1845 the Prussian Government asked the Oberburgermeister to investigate the feasibility of using the former Minorite monastery as a museum. However, a majority of the council preferred to build a new museum in the Trankgasse.

In the spring of 1849 Sulpiz Boisserée drew up plans for a museum, emphasizing the excellent site offered by the former monastery.

Planning difficulties were overcome when in 1854 the Cologne merchant Johann Heinrich Richartz (1795-1861) donated 100,000 thalers to the council for the construction of a museum, with the proviso that they use the city's most fashionable architect of the time, Josef Felten. The council did not hesitate to accept the offer on 3 August 1854, and joined Richartz's name to that of Wallraf to form the title of the new Museum. Improvements and enhancements were made to the plans by Julius Raschdorff, and the building that eventually arose on the site of the monastery was the fruit of a collaboration of both architects.

The new building (opened 1 July 1861) gave a home not only to the art collection but to the Cologne Society for the Arts, founded in 1839 for the promotion of contemporary art, and to the drawing school run by the painter Johannes Niessen (1821-1910), Ramboux's successor. The cloister housed Roman and medieval sculptures and Roman mosaics, while the upper storey housed the medieval stained glass donated by the Boisserée brothers. Plaster casts of famous sculptures were also planned for the new building. But from the beginning the emphasis of the Wallraf-Richartz Museum was on the painting gallery. So it was not surprising that the department of paintings expanded most rapidly and soon outgrew its accommodation.

Even before the collection had moved to its new home, there had been no dearth of new acquisitions. The first donations of paintings can be traced back to 1829. Purchases, gifts and bequests brought new and valuable additions to the collection. Stefan Lochner's *Virgin of the rose bower* finally came into the possession of the Museum as a gift from city councillor F. J. von Herwegh after having been on loan since 1828. But the real process of acquisition and building up the collection only began in earnest after the opening of the new premises in 1861. In 1860, despite considerable opposition from the city council, the Museum purchased *Prometheus bound* by Jacob Jordaens for 1,000 thalers from Dr E. Schenk. Before the city architect's collection went missing, the museum was able to buy, in 1862, Peter Paul Rubens's *Holy Family* for 5,000 thalers. At the beginning of that year, the museum acquired by purchase an altarpiece of *The Crucifixion* by the Master of St Bartholomew. The so-called Lyversberg *Passion* was the last major acquisition of Ramboux's period in office in 1864.

After Ramboux's death Johannes Niessen was appointed director in 1866; his curatorship saw the expansion of the collection in the areas of the Düsseldorf school and Flemish Baroque. In early 1890, however, Johannes Niessen was made to resign his post. The position of museum director had already been advertised on 16 May 1889; for the first time appropriate academic and scientific qualifications were demanded. This reflected a change in the concept of the function and status of the museum. Out of an impressive list of twenty-seven candidates, Carl Aldenhoven was appointed on 7 November 1889, with a pensionable salary of 6,000 marks.

The reorganization of the gallery was one of Aldenhoven's most important tasks in his early years as director. The prevailing disorder had not only been apparent to the city council but was the occasion for much complaint by foreign visitors. Another urgent task was the development of a systematic catalogue. Johannes Niessen had

The Wallraf-Richartz Museum around 1900

himself catalogued the exhibits, but in the form of lyrical descriptions of the objects, more poetic than scientific. The building extensions required for the reorganization of the Museum were undertaken between 1892 and 1904. The greatly increased stock of paintings had put pressure both on the Arts Society and on the drawing school. Although the paintings were hung frame to frame, covering the walls right up to the ceiling, the extension was still not large enough. So a second floor was added above the cloister. The collection was now organized into two main sections, painting of the Middle Ages in Cologne and late nineteenth-century painting. Reflecting the taste of that period, the department of plaster copies of Roman and Greek sculptures was also extended; in 1905 it was opened as a separate unit.

After Carl Aldenhoven's death in 1907 the city council moved rapidly to fill his post, and from twenty-three candidates, on the advice of Ludwig von Tschudi, Max Friedlander, Alfred Lichtwark and Wilhelm von Bode, the council appointed Alfred Hagelstange in 1908.

Hagelstange began his period of office with another reorganization of the Museum. In 1908 he put the collection of plaster sculptures into storage (much to the concern of the Rhenish curator of monuments, Paul Clemen), to gain more space for the paintings. He

The rebuilt Wallraf-Richartz Museum
around 1957

introduced the method of hanging paintings we know today, that is in a row next to each other and not densely covering the whole wall, one on top of the other.

The funds available to him from the city treasury for new acquisitions were very modest, but he nevertheless managed to win patrons and donors with his charm. He succeeded in acquiring around 90 paintings in his six years as director, including Vincent van Gogh's *Railway bridge* in 1911. In November of the same year he managed to secure for the Museum Hofrat Seeger's collection of works by Leibl for 1,050,000 gold marks. Cologne patrons contributed 332,000 gold marks. A year later he acquired the famous portrait of '*Mr and Mrs Sisley*' by Auguste Renoir and shortly before the outbreak of war *The Soler family* by Pablo Picasso (seized in 1937 as 'degenerate art'). His introduction of contemporary art into the collection was heavily criticized by the press and critics. (One of the most outspoken opponents of the Cologne director and his approach to collecting was the influential director general of the Berlin museums, Wilhelm von Bode.)

The First World War interrupted what were very promising developments for the Wallraf-Richartz Museum; the war and its consequences cut the Museum off from its contacts in the west and the death of its young director in December 1914 brought the life of Cologne's museums to a halt.

It was not until 19 December 1919 that the council appointed a new director to the empty post – Carl Schaefer from Lubeck. On 25 August 1921 the council decided to reorganize the Wallraf-Richartz Museum once more, together with the Museum of Decorative Arts. The idea – apparently developed by Schaefer – was to amalgamate the Wallraf-Richartz Museum's collection of early paintings (including the Renaissance) with the collection held by the Museum of Decorative Arts, for administrative purposes, without affecting their display. Schaefer became the director of this combined collection. The collection of Roman antiquities was to be under another curator, and the collection of medieval art was also entrusted to a specialist. The remainder of the collection, including the engravings, became a gallery of modern art. A new directorship for this Museum was established, to which Hans F. Secker from Danzig was appointed in 1922. The new reorganization again necessitated more building work. After many months of closure the Museum was reopened on 1 December 1923.

However, the new arrangement was not blessed with success; the number of visitors did not grow and that of exhibitions declined. The two directors worked in vain. Difficulties increased to the extent that Schaefer and Secker were continually selling off paintings, so that by October 1924 it was felt necessary to found a 'Society for the Protection of the Art Collections of the City of Cologne'. By 1927 the situation of the Cologne museums had deteriorated so far that a new approach was desperately needed. The view taken was that the division of the collection into two should be scrapped and that the seventeenth-century collection, until now neglected, should be strengthened. The new approach received a boost when the Carstanjen collection was acquired in summer 1928, though on loan. This set the path for future development and settled the issue of reuniting the collection.

On 1 October 1928 Oberburgermeister Konrad Adenauer drew a line under that episode of the Museum's history by appointing Ernst Buchner from Munich as director of a reunited gallery. Despite limited resources and his short period as director (until March 1933), he managed to make important acquisitions. He gave the Museum its present organizational structure. When Buchner was elected to be director general of the Bavarian state art collections in 1933, he was succeeded by Otto H. Förster as director of the Wallraf-Richartz Museum on 1 April.

Förster's first and most difficult task was to ensure that the Carstanjen collection remained in Cologne, and it was finally purchased in February 1936 for 2.2 million Reichsmarks. This seemed too high to some members of the city government and there was even talk of selling off to Amsterdam a Rembrandt self-portrait from the newly acquired collection – the idea was nevertheless quickly dropped.

Once again the Museum was completely reorganized. This settled the long standing demand for artificial lighting; all rooms were fully renovated and the walls were partly covered. Unfortunately, these positive developments for the Wallraf-Richartz Museum were abruptly broken off during the Third Reich. On 6 July 1937 a Reich commission led by the President of the State Committee for the Fine Arts, Adolf Ziegler, selected a considerable number of paintings and prints from the Department of Modern Art for the now infamous exhibition of 'degenerate art'. This exhibition initiated the confiscation of modern art held by public institutions, a loss that deprived the modern gallery of its European status.

During the Second World War, the Museum's collections were stored away, returning to the ruined city at the end of the war with very few losses. However, the Neo-Gothic museum building, already badly damaged by bombs, had been completely destroyed in an air raid on 29 June 1943.

After the end of the war, Otto H. Förster retired, and in his place Leopold Reidemeister was appointed director general for all the museums in Cologne.

While Cologne lay in ruins and the deliberations as how to rebuild continued, the city was bequeathed Josef Haubrich's valuable collection of works he had rescued during the years of state-directed art. The Museum was rebuilt on the site of the previous one, from 1953 to 1956, to a design by the architects Rudolf Schwarz and Josef Bernard. On 27 May 1957 the building was formally handed over to the city. In the following years the number of visitors increased and the collection could be expanded according to plan.

With the Haubrich gift, the department of twentieth-century art became an important collection in its own right. The acquisition of the Ludwig collection in October 1968 gave the department even more substance. For these reasons the council decided on 23 February 1976 to create a new museum of twentieth-century art – the Ludwig Museum. Since then the Wallraf-Richartz Museum's collection has consisted of three groupings, the painting of the Middle Ages, Renaissance and Baroque art, and nineteenth-century art. The graphic collection forms a separate, independent entity – a museum within the museum.

Shortly after the opening of the rebuilt Wallraf-Richartz Museum it became clear that the building had many inadequacies. The most serious mistakes were that the air-conditioning was limited to the main floor; the lateral illumination in the medieval department was too strong, and the graphics collection was unfavourably located in the

east wing. The circulation plan designed for the new museum building proved a hindrance to the meaningful hanging of the pictures. From his appointment in 1961, the new director, Gert von der Osten, tried assiduously to obtain a new building for the Wallraf-Richartz Museum. The acquisition of the Ludwig collection in 1968 speeded up the decision. After much controversy and debate, the site of a former bus station close by the cathedral was chosen, which in 1972 the city of Cologne made available for construction. In October 1975 a competition for the design of the new building was advertised, the outcome of which was finally decided by the competition jury on 30 January 1976. The winners were the Cologne architects Peter Busmann and Godfrid Haberer. Construction of the new building began on 28 January 1977, the official laying of the foundation stone by Oberburgermeister Norbert Burger followed on 26 January 1982 and the new museum was opened on 6 September 1986.

The new building complex of the Wallraf-Richartz Museum and the Ludwig Museum to the south-east of Cologne cathedral is part of the renovation of the old town, the heart of Cologne. A daring feature of the new building is its juxtapostion against the cathedral. Another feature is the close proximity of other important museums (the Römisch-Germanisches archaeological museum is also close by).

The new building with its flexible gallery divisions provided an opportunity to create a museum that differed significantly from the standard approach. The display of works of art – which these days is demanded of a museum – takes precedence over the traditional functions of collection and research. One aim of the interior design was to give the visitor an exciting journey into the realm of art. Varied sequences of rooms underpin this approach. The most important museum spaces open on to Museumsstrasse along the main axis from west to east. This grand gallery is the main route from which side routes branch off into the relevant rooms and display areas. Rooms of different sizes make the tour through the collections an appealing experience with continually changing viewpoints. Nevertheless the system is so designed that it enables the visitors to leave out single or whole groups of rooms if they are not interested in them. The staircase connects the collections of the Wallraf-Richartz Museum and the Ludwig Museum, a physical link that demonstrates to the visitor the connection between early and modern art. So that the staircase is not seen merely as a point of transition, large-scale Baroque paintings are hung on the walls. On the north side, directly reached from the stairs, are the rooms housing the medieval altarpieces. The majority of them exploit the play of natural daylight (from above and the side); flattening, artificial lighting was deliberately avoided.

This new museum concept has clearly been popular with the visitors. A gallery of famous paintings is there not only to serve the history of art but above all the city and the people who support it.

RAINER BUDDE
Director

View of the staircase providing access to
both the Wallraf-Richartz Museum and
the Ludwig Museum

The collection of medieval art

Medieval painting has been one of the most important features of the collection of the Wallraf-Richartz Museum since its inception. Comprising Italian, early Netherlandish and early German paintings, it is one of the greatest collections of its kind in the world. In the field of medieval painting from Cologne, it is unmatched in size and scope: all the masters and workshops, with a variety of themes and types of pictures and altarpieces, are represented here. Although most of the works come from the original Wallraf collection, the medieval holdings have constantly been expanded since 1824 through gifts and the purchase of both collections and individual pieces.

In its current form, the collection offers a good overview of the development of painting in the Middle Ages from 1280 (the Lucca *Madonna*) to the Mannerism of the Netherlands (Joos van Cleve) or to the early German Renaissance (Dürer, Burgkmair). The works here show the development of painting – the styles, themes, formats and techniques – over almost three hundred years. Pictures from Italy and Cologne illustrate the beginnings of the painted altarpiece from around 1300. The International Gothic style of around 1400 is represented by an outstanding series of paintings and altarpieces. There are very good examples of early realism from the Netherlands after the mid-fifteenth century. The broad range of Late Gothic painting – the autumn of the Middle Ages – enables the visitor to form an impression of the gamut of stylistic developments, from local traditionalism to the impact of foreign influences. The museum's wide-ranging collection contains instances of all the period's major developments, from the devotional image for private piety to the altar retable in the church; from the legends of the saints with their narrative richness to the portrait as a new form of self-presentation.

The reorganized galleries have given new life to the painting of the Middle Ages: its original functions are emphasized with free-standing and partly reconstructed altars. Through juxtapositions, influences and similarities between styles can now be more easily recognized, but also the differences between the painting of individual towns and regions are more apparent.

The painting of the Middle Ages was almost exclusively religious. The altarpieces were mostly commissioned and paid for by the clergy and the aristocracy. The pictures functioned as part of the church services, as well as to decorate the churches, but were also a product of concern about the afterlife. That is why on many altarpieces small figures of the donors are depicted, who by their virtuous demeanour and gift of the painting hope to secure indulgence for their souls. Information about the context of the paintings – as well as materials and techniques – which are unfamiliar to many today, is given in the interpretative displays in the gallery.

Italian painting in the Middle Ages

The small but very varied collection of medieval Italian art illustrates the most important features and relationships of the period. From the fourteenth century Italian medieval painting, hitherto strongly influenced by the Byzantine tradition, was particularly progressive (*e.g.* Giotto, Lorenzetti, Martini). It was instrumental in the development of perspective and composition, and is notable for its variety of types of image and for a new understanding of effects of colour.

In Italy, with its profound piety, images of Christ and the Virgin Mary were found from early on, in contrast to northern Europe. Altarpieces such as the Lucca *Madonna* were already common in the twelfth and thirteenth centuries. This cult image is strongly traditional and yet has elements of content and form that anticipate future developments. Opposite this almost transcendental picture is Simone Martini's *Virgin and Child*, showing a more sophisticated approach to the subject. Here, as in the Lorenzetti altarpiece, the profound relationship between mother and child, the reserved, majestic character and the subtle symbolism, as well as the novel sweetness and painterly handling are definite indications of a new era.

Italian art – particularly from Siena – played an important role in a new, international, Late Gothic style. Not only in the development of soft, gently flowing forms, with a new approach to the drapery and space, but also in the preoccupation with personal compassion and the human representation of Christ, the generation of Martini and Lorenzetti introduced a new approach to painting. The *Flagellation of Christ* by Giovanni di Pietro d'Ambrogio, painted on the case of an official document, and the Umbrian altarpiece of the *Man of Sorrows* are impressive and powerful examples of this art with its new spirituality, strongly influenced by monastic movements in the towns and also by terrible personal experiences of the plague. The panel of the *Man of Sorrows* is at the same time a plea for indulgence. Devotional images like these and Bicci di Lorenzo's *Nativity* serve as a personal call to prayer.

Part of the medieval collection in the Wallraf-Richartz Museum

17

1

Lucca, c1260
The Madonna enthroned with the Christ Child
Canvas laid over poplar, 104 × 63 cm
(112 × 71 cm including original frame)
Inv.no. Dep.319. On loan since 1968 from

the Neven DuMont family, Cologne
This panel, originally in the collection of
the painter Franz von Lenbach, shows
Mary as Queen of Heaven. The panel
was probably originally the centre of a
triptych or tabernacle.

1

2

Simone Martini
Siena 1280/85 – 1344 Avignon
The Virgin and Child, c1325-30
Poplar, 79.5 × 57 cm
Inv.no. WRM 880. Gift of the Land of
Nordrhein-Westfalen, 1961
This panel was originally the centre of a

polyptych, on the left of which was a
panel with St Geminianus and another
with St Michael, to the right panels
depicting St Augustine and St Catherine.
The altarpiece probably came from the
church of Saint Agostino, San
Gimignano.

1

Bicci di Lorenzo
Florence 1373–1452 Arezzo
The Nativity
Poplar, 88 × 58 cm
Inv.no. Dep.320. On loan since 1968
from the Neven DuMont family,
Cologne

Giovanni di Pietro d'Ambrogio
Siena 1409/10 – 1449 Siena
The Flagellation of Christ, 1441
Poplar, 45 × 30.5 cm
Inv.no. Dep.321. On loan since 1968 from
the Neven DuMont family, Cologne
This panel from the collection of Franz
von Lenbach was used as a case or cover

for documents belonging to Sienese tax
officials. The inscription gives the names
of the officials and their term of office,
from January to June 1441. Only four
coats of arms have been identified: Del
Gorgiera (left), Giovanelli (third from
left), Menghini (right), Bonelli (below
right).

2

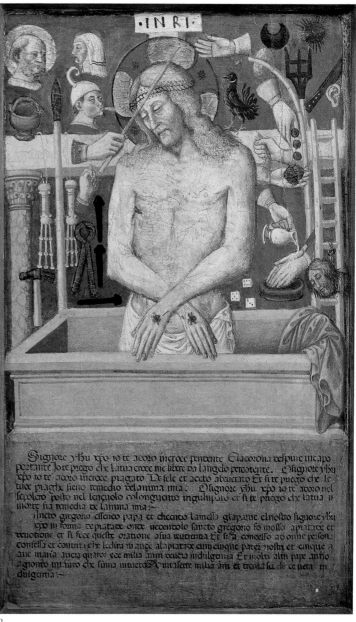

3

3
Umbria, last quarter of the
15th century
Christ as the Man of Sorrows, surrounded
by the *arma Christi*
Poplar, 79 × 47.5 cm
Inv.no. WRM 744. Transferred from the
Schnütgen Museum, Cologne in 1930

The text below the picture indicates the
purpose of the panel, a prayer for
indulgences, with the information that
any penitent who prays five Our Fathers
and five Hail Marys in front of this
painting will receive a total remission of
77,000 years and 36 days in Purgatory.

1

Ile de France, *c*1340-50
The Wehrdener *Crucifixion*
Oak panel, 169 × 111 cm
Inv.no. WRM 883. Purchased in 1964 with
the support of Westdeutsche Rundfunk,
the Volkswagenwerk Trust, the city of
Cologne and the Land of Nordrhein-
Westfalen

This panel was discovered as late as 1925
in Wehrden on the Weser and restored
in 1926. It is the work of an experienced
French artist, probably a wandering
painter, who seems to have learned the
Italian technique of perspective as well
as the courtly, elegant style flourishing
in Normandy.

1

2

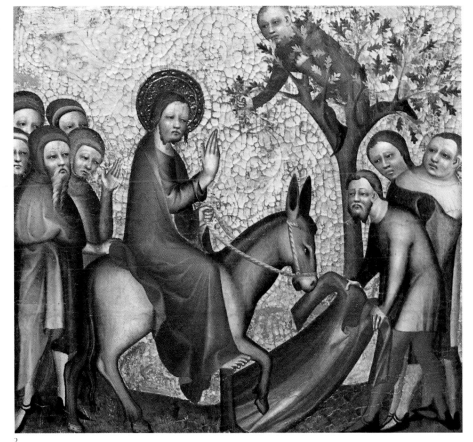

3

2 and 3
Westphalia, *c*1370-80
The Osnabrück altarpiece (centre panel)
Oak marouflaged on plywood in 1954,
117 × 262.5 cm
Inv.no. WRM 350. Acquired probably in
1842
This altarpiece is a typical example of
Westphalian painting of the late 14th
century. The composition of the central
panel is constructed like a triptych: the
accompanying images are to the same
scale as those of the wings (not shown).

Gothic and early modern painting in Cologne

In the Middle Ages, Cologne was one of the largest cities in Europe, with a population of around 42,000, and was also very wealthy because of its nodal position for traffic and its flourishing trade. Toll revenues, the right to mint coinage and special exemptions contributed to a constantly growing economy, while its international connections, as a member of the Hanseatic League, meant that Cologne's wares were distributed all over Europe. With numerous churches, monasteries, charitable foundations, chapels and hospitals, the 'holy city of Cologne' became known in medieval times as the 'Rome of the North'.

The views of the city preserved in Gothic painting (for example, in the work by the Master of the Assumption), show many towers on the skyline and a strong wall round the city. Thus a secure and wealthy Cologne provided fruitful conditions for the development of art during the early Middle Ages, as its increasing number of monasteries, churches and chapels all sought to decorate their altars. From about 1300 the city began to develop its own tradition in painting, one which lasted until around 1550. Cologne was therefore one of the most long-standing centres of art production in Europe.

In the fourteenth century painted altarpieces came to be preferred to the gilt statuary and mural painting hitherto in vogue, and some very interesting examples have survived. One of the most remarkable is a miniature altarpiece with wings depicting the *Life of Christ* which dates probably from the very beginning of painting in Cologne. Fragments of frescos with saints' heads from the town hall's Hansa chamber, the altar of the Clares (*c*1360-70) in Cologne cathedral, and the panels of the Misericordia altar illustrate its development during the fourteenth century. During the 'International Gothic' period from around 1395 to around 1425, Cologne was one of the leading centres of European painting, taking its artistic inspiration from the French court. Besides the workshop of the internationally important Master of St Veronica, there were numerous other successful shops in the city. Stefan Lochner, the most famous artist of medieval Cologne, probably came to the city from Lake Constance. After studying in the Netherlands he was influenced by the 'soft' or International Gothic style but then developed his own style of realism mixed with idealism, which he passed on to a wide circle of pupils and followers.

From the middle of the fifteenth century, painting in Cologne

1

came under the influence of Netherlandish art, which was spread by migrating artists and by the dissemination of portable works, and by the presence of key Netherlandish works in Cologne, including Rogier van der Weyden's Columba altar of about 1460, today in the Alte Pinakothek, Munich. The Master of the Life of the Virgin and his circle, the Master of the Holy Kinship, the Master of St Bartholemew, the Master of St Severin and the Master of the Ursula Legend may all have trained in different ateliers, but their works nevertheless consistently reflect the art of Rogier van der Weyden and Dieric Bouts. Characteristic of this phase is the increase in narrative painting, of realistic landscapes, towns and skies, as well as of portraits of individuals. With the arrival in Cologne in 1512 of Bartholomäus Bruyn the Elder from the Lower Rhine the Renaissance began, and is manifest particularly in portraiture.

3

3

2

Cologne, c1330

Winged altarpiece with the *Life of Christ*
Oak, centre panel 65 × 48 cm, each wing
65 × 24 cm
Inv.no. WRM1, Ferdinand Franz Wallraf
collection

From the evidence of the pious donor at
the foot of the Cross, this little altar
comes from the Cologne convent of the
nuns of St Clare. It is a private
devotional altar used for personal
meditation on the life and suffering of
Christ. The frame, the niches for
reliquaries and the rich punching of the
gold background show a link with the
goldwork for which Cologne was
famous. The style of drawing, with the
many gestures of the figures, connects
the work with Cologne manuscript
illumination around 1300. With its
articulated spaces, its use of highlights
to model figures and structures, and its
transparent colours this little altarpiece
represents the starting point of Gothic
painting in Cologne.

1

**The Master of St Lawrence
Active in Cologne c1415-30**
The Virgin in a paradise garden, c1420
Oak, 20.2 × 16.2 cm
Inv.no. Dep 361. On loan from the Peter
and Irene Ludwig collection, Aachen
This miniature devotional painting is
one of the key works of this master and
of Cologne painting of the *Weiche Stil* or
'soft style'.

2

Cologne, end of the 14th century
*St Elizabeth clothes the poor and tends the
sick*
Pine, 123.4 × 49.2 cm
Inv.no. WRM36. Ferdinand Franz Wallraf
collection
This panel was once the inside of the
right wing of an altarpiece. The outside
of the wing (also in the Museum) shows
the *Descent from the Cross*. With another
panel in the Wilhelm-Hack Museum,
Ludwigshafen, this is part of a
'Misericordia' altarpiece depicting the
Acts of Mercy, and probably once stood
in a hospital in Cologne.

3

**The Master of St Veronica
Active in Cologne c1395-1415**
Triptych, central panel of walnut
58.9 × 39.5 cm, each wing of oak
59.1 × 19.9 cm
Inv.no. WRM10. Ferdinand Franz Wallraf
collection
On the wings are St Catherine (left) and
St Barbara (right), turning towards the
centre panel with the famous Madonna
of the flowering sweetpea. The pea stem
– not a vetch as thought earlier – is an
unusual attribute symbolizing Mary's
virginity. This altarpiece is one of the
most important examples of the late
Gothic *Weiche Stil* or 'soft style'.

4 and 5

**The Elder Master of the Holy
Kinship
Active in Cologne c1410–40**
Triptych, *The Holy Kinship*
Oak, central panel 85.3 × 95 cm, each
wing 86.3 × 41 cm
Inv.no. WRM59. Ferdinand Franz Wallraf
collection
The depiction of the extended Holy
Family ('Holy Kinship') on the central
panel introduces one of the most
popular new themes for paintings at the
beginning of the 15th century. All
Christ's relatives are gathered together,
following a description in the *Golden
Legend* of 1263-73 by Jacopo da Voragine.

3

4

5

**The Master of the Wasservass
Calvary
Active in Cologne 1415-35**
The Passion of Christ, c1420-30
Oak panel, 131 × 180 cm
Inv.no. WRM65. Ferdinand Franz Wallraf
collection

The suffering of Christ is portrayed in
simultaneous scenes. The artist was
obviously concerned to emphasize
spatial qualities in the painting. The
panel was donated by the wealthy
patrician von dem Wasservass family to
the Cologne parish church of St
Columba.

**The Master of the Small Passion
Active in Cologne c1400-20**
*The martyrdom of St Ursula before the
city of Cologne, c1411*
Canvas, 60 × 179 cm
Inv.no. WRM51. Ferdinand Franz Wallraf
collection
Since St Ursula and her 11,000 virgins
had been venerated for over a thousand

1

2

years in Cologne, and she was a patron saint of the city, her martyrdom is not surprisingly depicted with an extensive view of Cologne. Many medieval monuments are identifiable in the painting. From these the painting can be dated to around 1411. This is the first generally accurate illustration of the important city of Cologne and one of the earliest German paintings on canvas.

3
Stefan Lochner
Meersburg c1400 – 1451 Cologne
The Virgin of the rose bower, c1451
Oak, 50.5 × 40 cm
Inv.no. WRM67. Acquired in 1848 as a gift from Herr F. J. von Herwegh
This painting is one of the most

beautiful and important devotional images of the Virgin Mary in the whole of Gothic art. It has an extraordinarily dense texture of theological symbolism. The colours are laid in with the finest brush in many transparent glazes, and the most precious pigments of gold and lapis lazuli are prominent.

3

1

1

Stefan Lochner
Meersburg c1400-1451 Cologne
The Last Judgement, c1435
Oak, 124.5 × 172 cm
Inv.no. WRM66. Ferdinand Franz Wallraf
collection
This panel probably once hung as an
illustration of Justice in the Cologne
town hall. Its iconography, style and
many details follow Netherlandish
models such as the *Last Judgement* in
Diest, Belgium. As Lochner is supposed
to have trained in Robert Campin's
workshop, he must have encountered
Netherlandish art and the work of the
van Eyck brothers.

2

Cologne, c1450-60
Twelve scenes from the Life of Christ
Canvas, 93.5 × 115.5 cm
Inv.no. WRM3606. Acquired in 1988 with
the aid of the KulturStiftung der Länder,
Berlin; the Board of the Wallraf-Richartz
Museum/Ludwig Museum, Cologne; the
Friends of the Wallraf-Richartz
Museum/Ludwig Museum, Cologne, and
numerous citizens of Cologne

3

The Master of the Assumption
Active in Cologne c1460-80
Sts Anne, Christopher, Gereon and Peter,
c1480
Oak, 133.3 × 146.7 cm
Inv.no. WRM120. Ferdinand Franz
Wallraf collection

The panel is clearly divided into two
zones: in the foreground are St
Christopher as patron saint of shippers
and merchants, St Gereon as patron
saint of Cologne, St Peter as patron saint
of Cologne cathedral and St Anne. In the
upper section of the painting is a
panorama of the city of Cologne, from
the Bayenturm in the south to St
Kunibert in the north. The view of the
city is extraordinarily accurate. The
panel may well have been commissioned
after Cologne had become a free town of
the Empire (1475) and may document the
city's self-consciousness. The artist
appears to have been a follower of the
school of Stefan Lochner and his style
shows a Netherlandish training in its
realistic detail.

2

3

1

2

1 and 2

The Master of the Legend of St George
Active in Cologne *c*1460-90
The St George altarpiece, *c*1460
Oak, central panel 124.5 × 167 cm, each
wing 124.5 × 77 cm
Inv.no. WRM114-118. Ferdinand Franz
Wallraf collection

This unusual altar is the first in Cologne
not to have Christ or the Virgin as its
subject but an individual saint, St
George. However, on the exterior of the
wing on the left is the Adoration of the
Christ Child with the donor Peter
Kannegieser and family, and on the right
the *Ecce Homo* with the donor's parents.

3

4

3
The Master of the Life of Mary
Active in Cologne c1460-90
The Triptych of Canon Gerhard ter
Steegen de Monte, central panel c1480,
wings c1490
Oak, central panel 144 × 99 cm, each
wing 142 × 44 cm
Inv.no. WRM136-138. Ferdinand Franz
Wallraf collection
Joseph of Arimathaea and Nicodemus
show the body of Christ to the faithful.
The donor is touching the Saviour's
hand. On the left wing is St Andrew with
some of the donor's nephews, on the
right is St Thomas with more of them.
The triptych comes from the Stiftskirche
of St Andrew in Cologne.

4
The Master of the Life of Mary and
the Master of the Lyversberg
Passion
Both active in Cologne c1460-90
Christ on the Cross with Mary, John and
Mary Magdalene, c1465-70
Oak, 86.4 × 72.9 cm
Inv.no. WRM125. Acquired in 1846

1

1
The Master of St Bartholemew
Active in Cologne *c*1480/85-1510
The St Thomas altarpiece, 1501
Oak, central panel 143 × 106 cm; each
wing 143 × 47 cm
Inv.no. WRM179. Bequest of Herr Carl
Stein
This dramatic interpretation of the
Miracle of St Thomas is set in a
supernatural sphere and is combined
with a depiction of the Holy Trinity. The
altarpiece was donated by the lawyer Dr
Peter Rinck to the Carthusian church of
St Barbara in Cologne, and is a major
work by the Master.

2 and 3
The Master of the Lyversberg
Passion
Active in Cologne 1460-90
Two wings of an altarpiece, known as
the Lyversberg Passion
Oak, each wing 93.5 × 68.4 cm
Inv.no. WRM143-150. Acquired in 1864
This altarpiece constituted the high altar
of the Carthusian church of St Barbara,
donated by the Cologne merchant
Johann Rinck and his son the lawyer Dr
Peter Rinck. Thence it came into the
Lyversberg collection. The painting
includes an echo of a work by Dieric
Bouts, which was then in the church of
St Laurenz in Cologne and is now in the
Alte Pinakothek in Munich.

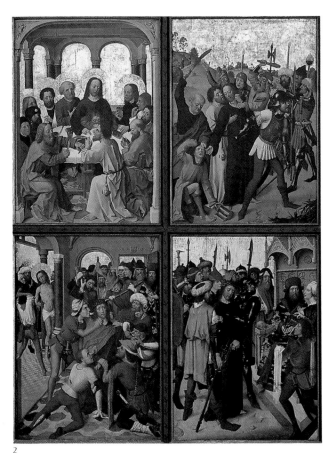

2

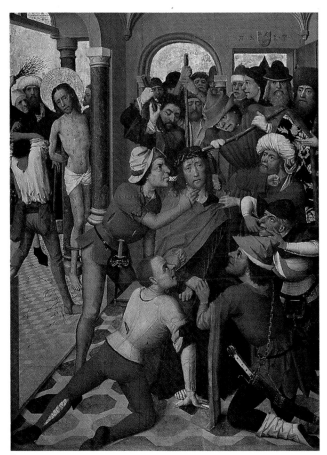

3

1

**The Master of the Holy Kinship
Active in Cologne *c*1480-1518**
The Holy Kinship altarpiece, *c*1505-10
Oak, central panel 144 × 187 cm; each
wing 144 × 88 cm
Inv.no. WRM165. Ferdinand Franz
Wallraf collection
The subject of Christ's relatives had
been very popular from the beginning of
the 15th century. On the left-hand wing
are Sts Nicasius and Roch with the
Cologne donor Nicasius Hackeney, who
ran the fiscal administration of the
imperial court; on the right are Sts
Gudule and Elizabeth with the donor's
wife, Christina (née Hardenrath). On the
exterior of the wings are Sts Hermolaus,
Achatius and his followers on the left,
and on the right Sts Cecilia, Genevieve,
Helen and Catherine, each with
members of the donor's family. The altar
was probably a donation to the
Dominican convent of St Achatius where
one of the donor's daughters was a nun.

2

3

4

2
The Master of St Bartholemew
Active in Cologne *c1480/85-1510*
Exterior of the wings of the Crucifixion altarpiece, 1495-1501
Oak, each wing 107 × 80 cm
Inv.no. WRM180. Acquired in 1862
These are early examples of grisaille painting in Cologne. The altarpiece was donated by Dr Peter Rinck for the rood screen of the Carthusian church of St Barbara between 1495 and 1501.

3
The Master of St Severin
Active in Cologne *c1480-1515/20*
The Adoration of the Magi, c1505
Oak, 57.2 × 50.7 cm
Inv.no. WRM3258. Acquired in 1975
In contrast to most of the large-scale and ceremonious images of the Magi in Cologne this small-format picture depicts an intimate and familiar scene. Idealism is combined with realistic observation.

4
The Master of St Severin and the
Master of the Ursula Legend
Both active in Cologne
c1480-1515/20
The St Francis altarpiece, c1500-05
Oak, central panel 132.5 × 163 cm, each wing 130.3 × 75 cm
Inv.nos. WRM193-194, WRM 531.
Ferdinand Franz Wallraf collection
The central panel shows St Francis receiving the stigmata, and also other scenes from his legend. On the left wing are Sts John Capistran and Bonaventura; on the right wing Sts Louis of Toulouse and Bernard of Siena (not illustrated). On the exteriors are St Francis and five Moroccan martyrs of the Order (not illustrated). This altarpiece is an important example of the iconography of St Francis and of Franciscan propaganda.

1

1

**The Master of the Ursula Legend
Active in Cologne** *c1480-1515/20*
Ursula with her parents at the altar,
1492-96
Canvas, 124 × 115 cm
Inv.no. WRM196. Acquired in 1895

This painting is the fourth in a cycle of
19 pictures of the legend of Ursula which
today are scattered throughout the
museums of Europe. Originally it was in
the Stiftskirche of St Severin in Cologne.

2

3

2
Anton Woensam von Worms
Worms before 1500 – before 1541
Cologne
Christ on the Cross with saints of the
Carthusian Order, 1535
Oak, 67 × 86.5 cm
Inv.no. WRM208. Given in 1857 by
J.J. Merlo
Canon Petrus Blomevenna, prior of the
Cologne Carthusians, is kneeling at the
foot of the Cross with members of the
Order at his side. The panel comes from
the Carthusian monastery of St Barbara
in Cologne. The painter, Anton
Woensam, was influenced by the
Cologne tradition as well as by Antwerp
Mannerism and Dürer.

3
Bartholomäus Bruyn the Elder
Wesel 1493 – 1555 Cologne
Burgomaster Arnold von Brauweiler, 1535
Oak, 57 × 38.5 cm
Inv.no. WRM243. Ferdinand Franz
Wallraf collection
With Bartholomäus Bruyn the Elder
portraiture was introduced to Cologne
and became a major new artistic genre.

Early Netherlandish painting

The Wallraf-Richartz Museum's collection of early Netherlandish paintings has been extensive since it was founded. After the middle of the fifteenth century, when the influence of Netherlandish art was widely felt in neighbouring countries, numerous important works of Netherlandish painting could be seen in Cologne's churches. Several key painters of the late Gothic style in Cologne – such as the Master of the Legend of St George or the Master of St Bartholomew – probably came from the Netherlands. This artistic exchange reflected a religious one: the archbishopric of Cologne, which included the suffragan bishoprics of Liège and Utrecht, extended into the Netherlands, whence in turn clerics, and spiritual movements such as the *devotio moderna* of Gerhard de Groote, came to Cologne.

The painting by the Master of the Catherine Legend of scenes from the Life of Job is an example both of the export of Netherlandish art and of the influence of Rogier van der Weyden and Dieric Bouts, whose narrative works and landscape backgrounds were eagerly used as models. In Jan Mostaert's *Holy Family at table* the traditional image of the Christ Child is integrated into an everyday setting and portrayed in new, intimate scenes. Such a step forward can only be explained by the increasing tendency to realism, accompanied by the development of secular imagery.

Quentin Massys and Jan de Beer were Netherlandish painters of the transition to the Renaissance, whose painterly invention and observation are well illustrated by the examples in the museum. In Jan de Beer's triptych of the *Adoration of the Shepherds* late-Gothic forms mix with Renaissance motifs. The same is true of Jacob von Utrecht's *Adoration of the Magi*, in which the Three Kings' adoration resembles the obeisance of a contemporary embassy, of a kind that must have been a common sight in Netherlandish towns around and after 1500. Quotations from the antique – the head of the king on the right recalls the head on a coin of Nero – are juxtaposed with traditional motifs and an extraordinarily precise observation of nature and life. Joos van Cleve, who apparently had great influence on many painters in Cologne and the Lower Rhine in his time, worked in the new style, although by preserving the old spirituality he avoided a sharp break with the past. Dating from the early sixteenth century, his triptych with the *Death of the Virgin* is a characteristic example of his art, setting out the old subjects with new relationships and iconography, but with painterly sensitivity.

1

1
Jan Mostaert
Haarlem (?) 1472/73 – 1555/56
Haarlem
The Holy Family at table, c1495-1500
Oak panel, 37.3 × 23.8 cm
Inv.no. WRM471. Acquired before 1862
This painting looks like a genre picture but the bread and wine indicate that these are Mary, Joseph and the Christ Child.

The Master of the Legend of St Catherine and the Master of the Legend of St Barbara
Both active in Brussels in the last third of the 15th century
Scenes from the Life of Job; (exterior) Job and St Mary Magdalen, c1480-90
Oak panel, 118.5 × 86 cm
Inv.no. WRM412. Acquired in 1889

This panel is the right wing of an altarpiece, which with three other pictures forms a triptych commissioned about 1480 by prior Claudio Villa (died before 1483), an Italian merchant in the Netherlands, for the Chapel of Job in Chieri, built by his brother Pietro Villa.

2

1
Quentin Massys
Louvain 1465/66 – 1530 Antwerp
John the Baptist and St Agnes, c1520
Oak, each wing 48 × 13.3 cm
Inv.no. WRM852. Acquired in 1936 with
the Carstanjen collection
The wings, which show Sts Lawrence
and Dorothy on their exterior, were
once part of a devotional triptych. The
centre is supposed to have been a Virgin
and Child crowned by angels.

2
Jan de Beer
Active in Antwerp 1490-1515
Triptych with the *Adoration of the
Shepherds*
Oak, central panel 73 × 56.3 cm, each
wing 76.4 × 24.5 cm
Inv.no. WRM.480. Given in 1980 by Dr
Hubert Dormagen Foundation, Cologne
On the left-hand wing is St Felicity with
her sons and on the right is St Ursula
with her followers. The composition and
style are characteristic of Antwerp
Mannerism of the early 16th century.

1

2

3
Jacob van Utrecht
Active in Lubeck and Antwerp
*c*1506-30
The Adoration of the Magi, *c*1513-20
Oak, 141 × 135 cm
Inv.no. WRM358. Franz Ferdinand
Wallraf collection
This panel is the front of the wing of an
altarpiece; on the reverse is St Bernard
of Clairvaux (not illustrated).

4
**Joos van Cleve the Elder (Joos van
Beke)**
Active in Antwerp 1511-40
Triptych with the *Death of the Virgin*
Oak, central panel 63 × 123.5 cm, each
wing 65 × 57 cm
Inv.no. WRM430. Ferdinand Franz
Wallraf collection
This altarpiece was originally in the
private chapel of the splendid Prager Hof
in Cologne, to which the donor Nicasius
Hackenay belonged and in which
Emperor Maximilian often stayed.

3

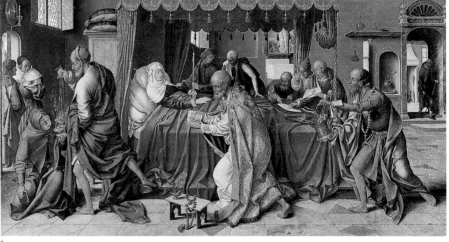

4

Early German painting

The collection of early German paintings is not very extensive but is of a high quality. Only Dürer's *Piper and drummer*, the right-hand exterior wing of the so-called Jabach altar, has long been in Cologne. The other paintings have been acquired by the Museum later as purchases or loans.

Near the end of the late Gothic period, the older art centres of both Germany and the Netherlands went into decline. Towns such as Antwerp and Nuremburg very quickly took over the leading role in the development and dissemination of the Renaissance style – not only in painting but also in other art forms. The main support for these developments came from an extensive network of humanist circles. Albrecht Dürer, who brought the new style to Nuremberg after his visits to Venice (1494-95 and 1505-07), became the founder of the South German Renaissance. The composition of figures in his paintings shows an exact observation of anatomy, an understanding of perspective and a new, vibrant use of colour. His study of the antique and of the Italian Renaissance was the foundation for his new imagery.

Lucas Cranach the Elder was influenced by Dürer early in his career but after 1505 he developed his own very individual style in a particularly extensive œuvre. As court painter to the dukes of Saxony in Wittenberg he was obliged to produce portraits but was also responsible for the decoration of churches. He had links with humanist thinkers and was friendly with Martin Luther, whom he often portrayed. His paintings in the Museum – *St Mary Magdalene*, a *Virgin and Child*, a portrait of a prince, the *Judgement of Paris* – are characteristic themes in his work. Cranach was particularly interested in the depiction of worldly and mythological subjects, and such works clearly show the importance for Cranach's art of the new Renaissance concept of beauty that emerged from the rediscovery of the antique.

Hans Burgkmair the Elder studied first in the Upper Rhine region with Martin Schongauer, and then settled in Augsburg in 1498. In 1503 he visited Cologne where he copied Stefan Lochner's *Last Judgement* in a drawing. He also visited Italy and Venice, where he learnt the principles of the new style. As a painter of both altarpieces and portraits, he is a transitional artist. Burgkmair made contacts at court and produced a series of woodcuts for Emperor Maximilian I; he became famous as a painter of outstanding portraits in the new style between 1490 and 1512.

The influential role of Italian art can also be seen in the work of Georg Pencz. Based in Nuremberg, of which he became the town painter in 1532, he was a follower of Dürer and is likely to have been trained in his workshop. The panels in the Museum show a great similarity with Dürer's style and have often passed for Dürer's work.

1

1

Georg Pencz
Leipzig c1500 – 1550 Leipzig
Angel, c1525-30
Limewood, 50.9 × 17 cm
Inv.no. 376. Acquired in 1865 with
funds from the Richartz Trust
This panel, together with three other
small paintings in the Museum of Sts
John the Baptist, John the Evangelist and
Christopher, was originally part of a
triptych, of which the central panel
might have been a *Crucifixion* or a
Virgin.

2

Albrecht Dürer
Nuremberg 1471 – 1528 Nuremberg
Piper and drummer, 1502-04
Limewood, 94 × 51.2 cm
Inv.no. WRM369. Ferdinand Franz
Wallraf collection
The panel, cut away at the top, is the
exterior of the right-hand wing of an
altarpiece, originally opposite a picture
of suffering Job on the dungheap (now in
the Städel'sche Museum, Frankfurt),
whose wife is dousing him with water.
The two musicians are trying to cheer
him up, as he lies abandoned by all in
his melancholy. The drummer is at least
partly a self-portrait by Dürer. The
interior wing panels are in the Alte
Pinakothek in Munich; the central panel
is lost. The altarpiece may have been
painted for Frederick the Wise in
Wittenberg. From the beginning of the
17th century it was in the private chapel
of the Jabachschen Hof in Cologne.

2

1

Hans Burgkmair the Elder
Augsburg 1473 – 1531 Augsburg
Barbara Schellenberger, 1505-07
Limewood, 41.5 × 28 cm
Inv.no. WRM851. Acquired in 1936 with
the Carstanjen collection

2

Hans Burgkmair the Elder
Augsburg 1473 – 1531 Augsburg
Hans Schellenberger, 1505-07
Limewood, 41.5 × 28 cm
Inv.no. WRM850. Acquired in 1936 with
the Carstanjen collection
Hans Schellenberger was an Augsburg
patrician, who married Barbara Ehem in
1506. He is holding an eyebright flower
in his hand, signifying cheerfulness; she
has a lily of the valley, a symbol of
future happiness. The inscriptions, the
portrait type, their being pendants, the
symbols and the age of the subjects
identify these as betrothal and marriage
portraits. These paintings, formerly in
the Hermitage in St Petersburg, are the
only surviving pair of portraits by
Burgkmair.

3
Lucas Cranach the Elder
Kronach 1472 – 1553 Weimar
The Judgement of Paris, c1512-14
Limewood, 43 × 32.2 cm
Inv.no. Dep. 322. On permanent loan
from the Neven DuMont family,
Cologne

This mythological theme was very
popular with the humanist-educated
bourgeoisie as well as the court and
Cranach the Elder painted it often. This
picture came from the Franz Lenbach
collection in Munich.

3

Flemish painting in the sixteenth and seventeenth centuries

An outstanding feature of the Netherlandish Baroque Masters collection of the Museum is its Flemish painting dating from about 1550 to 1650. Its holding of some sixty paintings is representative of all the major artists, types of picture, themes and genres of the southern Netherlands during this period.

Before the Golden Age of painting in newly independent Holland in the seventeenth century, with its individual city cultures, the old trading centres of Ghent, Bruges and, later, Antwerp had already seen a flowering of art. These southern towns were the traditional centres of art and culture, court and church, science and economy in the former Burgundian, then Habsburg-Spanish Empire. Even though today Netherlandish painting of the 16th and 17th centuries is rare in Cologne, there is evidence of its influence in the painting of nearby Cologne and the regions along the Rhine. Painting in our city has always reflected early Netherlandish and later Flemish styles and trends, from Hugo van der Goes to Rubens, from the Bruyn family to the Cologne artists of the seventeenth century. The connections extended across the whole range of art, from altarpieces to portraits. Trade and faith, economy and Church linked Cologne and the Netherlands inextricably both before and after the partition of the country into north and south finally sealed by the Peace of Westphalia in 1648.

The political confusion of the sixteenth century resulted in a huge number of religious and economic refugees, including artists and craftsmen, who settled not only in Amsterdam but also in Cologne and along the Lower Rhine in addition to small enclaves, like Frankenthal and Frankfurt. Perhaps the most famous of those emigrants linked with Cologne was the master of Flemish and European Baroque painting, Peter Paul Rubens. He was born in Siegen in 1577 and his family lived in Cologne until his twelfth year; his father, Jan, died there in 1587. The commission for the altarpiece of the *Crucifixion of St Peter* (c1638), still *in situ* today, bears witness to Rubens's links to Cologne. Cornelis Schut (1597-1655) and Gerard Seghers (1591-1651) were also employed by the city, and the painter Geldorp Gortzius, having accompanied the Italian duke Terranova to Cologne in 1579, was another to settle here. He produced not only the *Christ on the Cross* for the council chamber in the tower of the town hall, but above all numerous portraits of Cologne patricians and citizens.

Despite the dissolution of churches and monasteries in the eighteenth century and the sales, losses and destructions of the twentieth, which decimated the collection of Flemish painting, the works in the Museum amount to a significant panorama of masters and themes. From the original Wallraf collection comes Joachim Beuckelaer's *Nativity* (believed by Wallraf to be by Bassano), Joos de Momper's *Mountain scene with bridges*, Kerstiaen de Keuninck's *Abduction of Ganymede*, the family portrait of Cornelis de Vos, and Rubens's *Stigmatization of St*

Francis. During the nineteenth and twentieth centuries the Museum often acquired masterpieces by the purchase of single works or of whole collections (for example the Carstanjen collection in 1936), including works by Rubens, Jordaens, Snyders, de Crayer and Teniers the Younger.

The selection presented here also includes artists such as Pieter Aertsen, Joachim Beuckelaer and Jacques de Gheyn II, sixteenth-century artists who for different reasons can be regarded as members of the Antwerp school. Although Aertsen and De Gheyn were also registered as members of the guild of painters in Amsterdam and The Hague, on the basis of their origins and style they have always been categorized as Flemish painters. Pieter Aertsen's *Market scene* embodies the transition from narrative to genre and then to still life. Equal weight was given to realistic genre and religious symbolism in the work of his nephew Joachim Beuckelaer.

This development from figurative painting to still-life painting is one of the great achievements of Flemish art, which, though it has many parallels with Italian Renaissance painting, independently reached unsurpassed heights. Frans Snyders, born the son of an innkeeper and wine merchant in Antwerp in 1579, in this category is one of the greatest virtuosos of the Baroque. He was not only friendly with Rubens but also painted the animals in many of his pictures.

A second historically significant development was in landscape painting, which became the basis of Dutch painting and the model for all forms of landscape until late into the nineteenth century. Flemish artists were responsible for the development of near and distant views and colour perspective. They also formulated the *Weltlandschaft* or 'bird's eye view' landscape and the principle of variety in combining mountains and streams, forests and villages. In comparison a painter like Kerstiaen de Keuninck, who came from Kortrijk and worked in Antwerp, seems in his *Landscape with the Abduction of Ganymede* backward-looking and old fashioned.

The career of the brothers Matthäus and Paul Bril was quite different. They made their way to Rome early on in their careers and in the Holy City rose to be the first great northern painters of pure landscape. The diversity and range of landscape and his sophisticated use of colour – browns, greens and blues – characterize the work of Joos de Mompers, ten years younger than the Bril brothers. His landscapes mark the end of an era of development. A new branch of Flemish landscape painting was to blossom with Rubens and Jan Wildens perhaps through Lucas van Uden.

The peak of the Flemish achievement was reached by three artists who are numbered among the greatest exponents of international Baroque, Peter Paul Rubens, Anthony van Dyck and Jacob Jordaens. Rubens's youth and training, until he became Freemaster of the Guild of St Luke in Antwerp, was influenced by

Pieter Aertsen
Amsterdam 1508 – 1575 Amsterdam
Market scene
Oak, 127 × 85 cm
Inv.no. WRM1022. Acquired in 1914

This painting has a multiple theme. The abundance of the market could be at the same time a representation of the Four Elements and an allegory of the Five Senses. Also, the market woman is being pestered by a bird-catcher, who is gripping a duck round the neck with obvious erotic overtones – as well as a realistic representation the painting is also a moral lesson, extolling moderation and restraint in contrast to the physical and sensual pleasures offered, for instance, in the plumpness of the fruit. In other paintings Aertsen introduced a religious scene in the background by way of admonition.

1

a revival of the rich traditions of the old Antwerp school. After 1585 the economic and political restoration of churches and guilds led to the rebuilding of destroyed altars and a boom in commissions. Rubens lived in Italy from 1600 to the end of 1608, where he devoted himself to the study of the antique, of humanism and of contemporary Italian art. The significance of this cultural tour for Rubens can clearly be seen in a portrait of a group of friends which is one of the jewels of the Museum's collection. This self-portrait with a circle of friends from Mantua is both autobiography and manifesto, a painting that refers to his years in Italy and to his Mantuan circle of friends in a most suggestive composition.

Anthony van Dyck's *Jupiter and Antiope* has a connection with Rubens, since it is from his early period, immediately before or shortly after his entry into Rubens's workshop. It appears as one among at least eight versions of the subject, including drawings and etchings, in the inventory of Rubens's goods.

To such conspicuous elegance of form and composition the work of the third great Flemish artist, Jacob Jordaens, is in complete contrast. Jordaens also came from Antwerp and, since he lived long, after Rubens's death became the foremost master of Flemish Baroque painting, together with Teniers the Younger, the great master of genre pictures at the end of the century. Both artists represent the robust vitality of folklore and the peasant and bourgeois element in Flemish art during the second half of the century. Between mythology, religion and the everyday they discovered a rich mine of artistic themes which grafted Italian and courtly influences on to strong native roots going back to Pieter Bruegel the Elder.

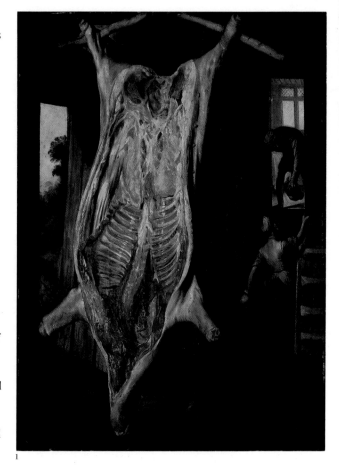

1

2

1

Joachim Beuckelaer
Antwerp c1530 – 1573/74 Antwerp
A slaughtered pig, 1563
Oak, 114 × 83 cm
Inv.no. WRM2324. Given by Herr
Hermann Neuerburg, Cologne
The theme of the slaughtered pig and the
tradition of the Netherlandish butchers'
shop were probably established by
Aertsen, who painted many such
pictures. The genre continued until
Rembrandt and beyond. It is also
supposed to have a religious
significance, as an allegory of the
Crucifixion and the Eucharist,
represented respectively by the pig in
the foreground and the wine being
brought from the cellar in the
background.

2

Jacques de Gheyn II
Antwerp 1565 – 1629 The Hague
Neptune and Amphitrite
Canvas, 103.5 × 137 cm
Inv.no. WRM1792. Ferdinand Franz
Wallraf collection
This half-length depiction of the married
sea gods whose love is symbolized by
the Cupid and the shells that accompany
them was originally described in
Wallraf's collection as 'Italian'. He was
deceived probably by the decorative
elegance of its colour and line, and by
the type of the double half-length, which
originated in Italy.

1
Paul Bril
Antwerp 1554 – 1626 Rome
Mountain scene, c1599
Copper, 11.8 × 17.5 cm
Inv.no. WRM3178. Acquired in 1964
The brothers Matthäus and Paul Bril
developed the art of depicting landscape
in terms of zones, established by colour
and by compositional structure, on
miniature, finely painted copper tablets.
Such motifs as cliffs, waterfalls, bridges,
chapels and paths are held together on
the diagonal and rendered convincing by
inserted figures of wanderers, riders and
hunters.

2
Paul Bril
Antwerp 1554 – 1626 Rome
Coastal landscape, 1596
Copper, 11.7 × 17.4 cm
Inv.no. WRM3179. Acquired in 1964

3
Joos de Momper
Antwerp 1564 – 1635 Antwerp
Mountain scene with bridges, c1600
Oak, 53 × 71.7 cm
Inv.no. WRM1019. Ferdinand Franz
Wallraf collection
These distinctively contoured vistas,
punctuated by tiny figures in the
foreground, and terminating in
colourful, increasingly transparent
backgrounds, are unmistakably Momper.
Distance, scale and breadth – a
sensibility that could be called romantic
– are combined here with the traditions
of earlier Flemish landscape art.

1

2

3

4

**Kerstiaen de Keuninck the Elder
Courtrai c1560 – 1635 Antwerp**
*Landscape with the Abduction of
Ganymede*
Oak, 69 × 121.5 cm
Inv.no. WRM1486. Ferdinand Franz
Wallraf collection
Characteristic of Keuninck are fantastic,
inpenetrable landscapes with often
wildly romantic backdrops of cliffs,
forests and trees. The picture is justified
by its mythological theme, here Jupiter
and Ganymede, as in the work of
Bruegel the Elder.

4

1

Peter Paul Rubens
Siegen 1577 – 1640 Antwerp
Self-portrait in a circle of friends from
Mantua
Canvas, 77.5 × 101 cm
Inv.no. Dep. 248. On loan from the
German government since 1961

2

Peter Paul Rubens
Siegen 1577 – 1640 Antwerp
The stigmatization of St Francis
Canvas, 382 × 243 cm
Inv.no. WRM1043. Ferdinand Franz
Wallraf collection
This picture was commissioned for the
high altar of the Capuchin church on
Machabaerstrasse in Cologne,
consecrated in 1616. Given to Wallraf in
1800 by the Capuchins to protect it from
the French, the painting remained in the
Wallraf collection when the monastery
was dissolved and the church destroyed.
The tall format of the painting makes it
likely to have been one panel of a fixed
retable – originally an Italian feature
adopted for altars north of the Alps
particularly during the Baroque period.
The style of the altarpiece, with its
emphatic single figure, was developed
further by Rubens shortly afterwards in
his designs for the altarpieces of St
Ignatius and St Francis Xavier for the
Jesuit church in Antwerp, and was
highly influential.

1

2

3

3
Peter Paul Rubens
Siegen 1577 – 1640 Antwerp
Juno and Argus, c1611
Canvas, 249 × 296 cm
Inv.no. WRM1040. Given in 1894 by the
Cologne Friends of Art
Rubens's study of the antique and of the
new sciences manifests itself in this
huge celebratory work which uses the
story of Jupiter's love for Io and the
jealousy of his wife Juno as an allegory
of the cosmos and demonstrates his
colour theory.

1
Osias Beert the Elder
Antwerp c1580 – 1624 Antwerp
Still life
Oak, 51.5 × 85.5 cm
Inv.no. WRM2584. Acquired in 1936

2
David Teniers the Younger
Antwerp 1610 – 1690 Brussels
Village scene
Oak, 29.4 × 25.5 cm
Inv.no. WRM2538. Acquired in 1936 with
the Carstanjen collection

1

2

3

3
David Teniers the Younger
Antwerp 1610 – 1690 Brussels
The Temptation of St Anthony, after 1640
Oak, 52.5 × 81.5 cm
Inv.no. WRM1029. Acquired in 1875

The temptations or trials of St Anthony,
who was tormented by spectres, witches
and devils while living as a hermit
among the barren cliffs, had often been
depicted in Netherlandish painting. The
basic type with mountain cliffs and
fantastic figures in human and animal
forms shows a clear relationship to
Bosch and Bruegel. As well as peasant
scenes, landscapes and mythology,
Teniers had an interest in depicting
ghosts, witches and alchemists.

4

5

4
Frans Snyders
Antwerp 1579 – 1657 Antwerp
Still life with a basket of fruit
Oak, 99 × 156 cm
Inv.no. WRM1350. Acquired in 1895
Snyders's usually large canvases and
panels are characterized by an

abundance of birds, game, fruit, fish,
meat and vegetables in a lively
arrangement. The exact representation
of the texture of feathers, fur and skin,
as well as the luminous, powerful
colouring in his later works are
outstanding.

5
Frans Snyders
Antwerp 1579 – 1657 Antwerp
Still life with poultry and game, 1614
Oil on canvas, 156 × 218 cm
Inv.no. WRM2894. Acquired in 1953

1

2

1
Anthony van Dyck
Antwerp 1599 – 1641 London
Jupiter and Antiope
Canvas, 112.5 × 151 cm
Inv.no. Dep.278. On loan since 1966
from the German government.
This mythological painting, in which
Jupiter seduces Antiope in the form of a
satyr, reveals the influence of Rubens's
monumental figures on van Dyck's early
style. The composition recalls the long
tradition of the sleeping nude, which
had classical precedent in the Vatican
Sleeping Ariadne and a Renaissance
interpreter, above all in Titian.

2
Gaspar de Crayer
Antwerp 1584 – 1669 Ghent
Alexander and Diogenes
Canvas, 196 × 278 cm
Inv.no. WRM1413. Acquired in 1869
The meeting between the classical ruler
Alexander the Great and the philosopher
Diogenes had been illustrated in the 15th
and 16th centuries but was also a
popular subject in Italian and
Netherlandish Baroque painting.
Diogenes replied to Alexander, the
conqueror of the world, when he asked
him if he wanted anything: 'Stand a little
less between me and the sun.' The
contrast between the youthful and
beautiful hero and the beggarly old man
whose life exemplified asceticism is
exploited in the composition and use of
colours. The message of the painting is
the meaninglessness of earthly power
when confronted with ethical principles.
The Antwerp artist de Crayer later
became court painter to the Archduke in
Brussels. This work, reflecting his
dealing with forms and themes in the
work of Rubens, is one of his best.

3
Jacob Jordaens
Antwerp 1593 – 1678 Antwerp
Prometheus bound, c1640
Canvas, 245 × 178 cm
Inv.no. WRM1044. Acquired in 1860
Jordaens's painting is a variation on a
theme that Rubens attempted early in
his career and which derived formally
from studies by Michelangelo.

3

Dutch painting of the seventeenth century

The collection of seventeenth-century Dutch painting in the Museum has been acquired mostly as gifts or loans from individual collectors, and by purchase since the second half of the nineteenth century. At that time there was a particular interest in the 'Golden Age' of Dutch painting: Rembrandt, Frans Hals and Jan Vermeer were 'rediscovered' and hailed as forerunners of nineteenth-century French realism.

Dutch painting of the seventeenth century was the artistic expression of a civil republic which for 80 years had fought the Spanish empire for its independence, finally recognized in the Peace of Westphalia in 1648. The astonishingly vast number of paintings, drawings and prints, as well as the invention of new artistic genres, are evidence of a cultural and economic boom and a new national consciousness which was reflected in the Dutch artists' choice of aspects of their homeland – the sea, the towns, the villages, their countrymen and even animals – as subjects.

Their paintings were regarded as solid and craftsmanlike, and their content was easily accessible, making them very popular with middle-class collectors in the nineteenth century. This may have been why the merchant Wilhelm Adolf von Carstanjen (1825-1900), born in Duisburg, resident in Cologne and then Berlin, started collecting masterpieces of Dutch painting in 1854. His collection now forms the core of the museum's collection of Dutch art. Accumulated over almost half a century, it contains three paintings by Rembrandt, including his famous late self-portrait, two portraits by Frans Hals, works by Teniers and Steen, and a range of representative works of Dutch landscape and portrait painting. After a chequered history, the collection came to the museum on loan in 1928 and in 1936 was purchased by the city of Cologne, preempting a planned sale to the city of Düsseldorf by Carstanjen's heirs.

Dutch painting of the seventeenth century is notable for the lack of commissions from the ecclesiastical and aristocratic patrons of the kind that characterize art in the rest of Europe. Of course artists were still commissioned – works for the civic authorities and the military, portraits of people and ships and marine views, such as those by Hendrick Cornelisz Vroom and van der Velde – but the majority of paintings were sold on the open market, through art dealers, bookshops, markets and the artists' own studios.

Artistic production in the Netherlands was determined by the demands of councillors, patricians, merchants and even farmers and fishermen. The Calvinist Church commissioned at the most church organs, pulpits, or funerary monuments, and the court of the Stadtholder (Governor) of the new republic in the Hague with its modest requirements for works of art could not compete with the royal courts of Europe. Only the third governor, Frederick Henry (ruled 1625-47), influenced by his art-loving secretary Constantijn Huygens, became a considerable builder and collector, though mainly of Flemish art. For the interior decoration of his palaces he employed history painters from Haarlem and Utrecht who were well versed in international court Baroque, such as Gerrit van Honthorst and Hendrick ter Brugghen.

Although Calvinists objected to any pictorial decoration in their churches, there was still a demand for private devotional images. Rembrandt is one of the great masters of religious history painting and was particularly outstanding with Old Testament subjects.

Secular figure painting, given the French label of genre painting in the eighteenth century, is one of the most characteristic and original types of Dutch painting. Genre painting took the most varied forms, from the peasant scenes of the followers of Pieter Bruegel the Elder to military scenes; from musicians, card-players and carousers to the social gatherings and interiors of the upper middle classes. The 'haute bourgeois genre', or 'geselschap', is a Dutch invention and first appears in the 1620s in the work of the Rotterdam artist Willem Buytewech, and then in the work of the Haarlem painters Dirck Hals, Pieter Codde and Willem Duyster. Antonie Palamedesz's *Party scene with music* shows just such a social gathering with wine, women and song.

There were also many and varied developments in portrait painting. Individual portraits in different sizes were produced as well as a type of group portrait peculiar to the northern Netherlands (for example of governors, militias and anatomy lessons) and family portraits. In portraits of married couples, the husband was almost always on the left and the wife on the right, sitting or standing, as in the portrait of a couple by the Haarlem artist Frans Hals, best known for his militia commissions. There were standard, pre-painted poses for portraits that the individual could choose, leaving the artist only to fill in the head. Even Rembrandt was dependent on this kind of portrait painting for money early in his career in Amsterdam, and many of his bust portraits cannot disguise the look of a production line.

If portraits give us an idea of what Dutch citizens looked like, the Wallraf-Richartz Museum's richly representative collection of landscape painting gives us a graphic view of the Dutch coastline, of its dunes, polders, forests and perennial cloudy sky. Dutch landscape painting depended on the Netherlandish tradition of the sixteenth century, but the direct access of the artists to their home environment is a new development, which goes together with a rejection of the traditional biblical and mythological figures that used to inhabit landscapes. Close views of specific landscapes with a low horizon, produced in Haarlem and later in Amsterdam, took over from the long-distance general views of the sixteenth century. In the 1620s, first by Pieter de Molijn and then Jan van Goyen and Salomon van Ruysdael, landscape space was set out along a diagonal and the standard composition graduated by

Hendrick ter Brugghen
Deventer 1588 – 1629 Utrecht
Bagpipe player, 1624
Canvas, 101 × 83 cm
Inv.no. WRM2613. Acquired in 1938

Like Honthorst, Hendrick ter Brugghen
was one of the major exponents of the
'Caravaggist' Utrecht school, with its
Italian images of flute, lute and bagpipe
players.

1
Hendrick ter Brugghen
Deventer 1588 – 1629 Utrecht
Bagpipe player, 1624
Canvas, 101 × 83 cm
Inv.no. WRM2613. Acquired in 1938

colour zones was abandoned, leading to a convincing naturalism in depictions of the flat Dutch landscape, giving due importance to the key element – the sky. Jan van Goyen pursued an almost monochrome style of painting, which showed an especially subtle sensitivity to the harmony of colour tones. The beauty of the northern Netherlands in different seasons and weathers is brilliantly captured in these paintings.

While this near realism of specific landscapes was the artistic goal until around 1650, after that time a new Baroque heightening of expression occurred, as can be seen particularly in the work of Jacob van Ruisdael, leading to a reintroduction of lively colour. Waterfalls were now depicted as dramatic, natural forces threatening man, while calm, evening sea-pictures were given a strange mystical quality in the work of Jan van de Capelle. Jan Hackaert's *River scene* and Frederick de Moucheron's *Mountain scene* clearly show a transition to the new international style of an ideal, classical landscape, which became the model for Dutch landscape painting until the end of the century and signified the end of its independent identity.

The still life also developed from sixteenth-century Netherlandish tradition, but then took a multiplicity of forms, with many sub-genres. There were specialists for flowers, for kitchen and market subjects, for the 'breakfast' still life, for 'tobacco pictures' and for hunting still lifes, to name but a few. Still-life painting was particularly suited to a display of the technical ability of the artist in the realistic representation of a variety of surfaces and textures. One master of this genre was Willem Claesz Heda, after Pieter Claesz a major exponent of the monochrome 'banketjes' (little breakfast) in Haarlem. The dominant grey-brown and olive-green palette of these paintings shows the small selection of objects to great effect and makes them look especially precious. While Heda was an important figure in Haarlem in still-life painting, this position in Amsterdam was filled by Willem Kalf. From the middle of the century, he specialized in portraying displays of magnificence which he painted with great skill and a feeling for the qualities of the precious metal utensils in ever new variations. These artificial arrangements and the sophisticated use of colour seem to lack the moral dimension which underlay many flower and breakfast still lifes at the beginning of the century.

A unique feature of Dutch architecture and interior decoration was the new genre of painting in Delft from the middle of the century, the church interior. Formerly only known in the work of Pieter Saenredam, it was developed in Delft almost simultaneously by the painters Gerrit Houckgeest, Hendrick van Vliet and Emanuel de Witte.

The works of the Dutch masters in the Museum show in their variety of type and artistic qualities a vivid picture of the culture of the Netherlands in the seventeenth century. Despite the allegorical and moralistic functions of genre painting, of which modern scholarship has become increasingly aware, the pictures lose nothing of their immediacy.

1

2

Hendrick Avercamp
Amsterdam 1585 – 1634 Kampen
Winter landscape, c1605-10
Oak, 25 × 34 cm
Inv.no. WRM1319. Ferdinand Franz
Wallraf collection
Hendrick Avercamp's early *Winter
landscape,* with its general view and
colourful narrative character, is very
much in the tradition of the famous
winter landscapes by Pieter Bruegel the
Elder. But Avercamp's winter landscapes
painted after the 1620s – reflecting the
trends of the period – are composed
with the now fashionable low horizon
and vanishing-point perspective.

2
Hercules Seghers
**Haarlem 1589/90 – after 1633 The
Hague**
View of Brussels from the north-east,
c1625
Oak, 24.5 × 39 cm
Inv.no. Dep.243. On loan since 1961 from
the German government

3
Esias van de Velde
Amsterdam 1587 – 1630 The Hague
Winter landscape, 1629
Oak, 11.2 × 14.9 cm
Inv.no. WRM2623. Acquired in 1941

4
Jan Victors
**Amsterdam 1619 – after 1676 East
Indies**
Esther and Haman before Ahasuerus,
c1638-40
Canvas, 128 × 169.5 cm
Inv.no. WRM1016. Acquired in 1879

5
Antonie Palemedesz
Delft 1601 – 1673 Amsterdam
Party scene with music, c1635-40
Oak, 64.5 × 89.5 cm
Inv.no. WRM1058. Given in 1840 by Herr
Friedrich von Ammon, Kleve, Cologne

1

2

3

64

4

5

1

Frans Hals
Antwerp *c*1582/83 – 1666 Haarlem
Portrait of a man, *c*1640
Canvas, 120 × 95 cm
Inv.no.2529. Acquired in 1936 with the
Carstanjen collection

2

Isaack van Ostade
Haarlem 1621 – 1649 Haarlem
Farmhouse interior, 1642
Oak, 50 × 68 cm
Inv.no. WRM3154. Acquired in 1963
Isaack van Ostade, like his brother
Adriaen, depicted peasant and low-life
scenes. This untidy farmhouse interior is
typical of Haarlem painting in the first
half of the 17th century, with its low-key
use of colour. The painting would be
taken as a warning against a dissolute
life.

1

2

3
Frans Hals
Antwerp c1582/83 – 1666 Haarlem
Portrait of a woman, c1640
Canvas, 120 × 94.5 cm
Inv.no.2530. Acquired in 1936 with the
Carstanjen collection

4
Simon de Vlieger
Rotterdam c1600 – 1653 Weesp
Beach near Scheveningen with fish-sellers,
c1643
Canvas, 47 × 71.7 cm
Inv.no. WRM1828. Given in 1898 by Frau
Peter Fuchs, Cologne

3

4

1

2

1
Rembrandt van Rijn?
Leyden 1606 – 1669 Amsterdam
Johannes Cornelisz Sylvius (?), 1644
Canvas, 126 × 103 cm
Inv.no. WRM2527. Acquired in 1936 with
the Carstanjen collection

2
Rembrandt van Rijn?
Leyden 1606 – 1669 Amsterdam
The Flagellation, c1646
Oak, 34 × 25.8 cm
Inv.no. WRM2528. Acquired in 1936 with
the Carstanjen collection

3
Gerrit Dou
Leyden 1613 – 1675 Leyden
Old woman with a candle, 1661
Oak, 31 × 23 cm
Inv.no. WRM2569. Acquired in 1936 with
the Carstanjen collection
This painting by the pupil of Rembrandt
and founder of the Leyden school of
'fine painting' represents a type common
in Leyden from the mid-1640s: the bust
portrait of an allegorical figure in an
architectural frame. Here the old woman
is shielding a candle flame, symbol of
the transience of human life.

3

4

4
Rembrandt van Rijn?
Leyden 1606 – 1669 Amsterdam
Self-portrait, c1668-69
Canvas, 82.5 × 65 cm
Inv.no. WRM2526. Acquired in 1936 with
the Carstanjen collection
This work comes at the end of a long
series of self-portraits, of which the
painter never seemed to tire. Painting
shortly before his death in 1669,
Rembrandt depicts himself as a laughing
grey old man at the easel. The uneven
preservation and the dark colour – what
the objects at the edges are can only be
guessed at – make the interpretation
very difficult. Most likely is the
explanation that Rembrandt has
portrayed himself in the role of the
ancient painter Zeuxis, who died
laughing while painting an ugly woman,
a story that Rembrandt's pupil, Aert de
Gelder certainly knew and contrasted
with the better-known legend that
Zeuxis had combined the best features
of the five most beautiful girls he could
find in order to produce a still more
beautiful image of Helen of Troy.

1
Allart van Everdingen
Alkmaar 1621 – 1675 Amsterdam
Forest scene with water-mill, c1650
Canvas, 73 × 61.5 cm
Inv.no. WRM1025. Given in 1888 by Herr
Dagobert Oppenheim, Cologne

2
Salomon van Ruysdael
Naarden 1600/03 – 1670 Haarlem
River scene with farmstead, 1647
Oak, 70.2 × 92.3 cm
Inv.no. WRM3117. Given in 1961 by
Klöckner-Humboldt-Deutz AG, Cologne

3
Jan van de Capelle
Amsterdam 1626 – 1679 Amsterdam
Calm, c1650-55
Oak, 47.5 × 59 cm
Inv.no.2535. Acquired in 1936 with the
Carstanjen collection

4
Jan van Goyen
Leyden 1596 – 1656 The Hague
River scene, 1652
Canvas, 66.7 × 98 cm
Inv.no. WRM1017. Acquired in 1897 with
funds from Herr Johann Wilhelm
Nakatenus, Cologne

1

2

3

4

1

1
Willem Kalf
Rotterdam 1619 – 1693 Amsterdam
Still life with silver bowl, glasses and
fruit, 1658
Canvas, 48.5 × 59 cm
Inv.no. Dep.490. On loan from a private
collection since 1985

2
Willem Claesz Heda
Haarlem 1594 – 1680 Haarlem
Still life, 1632
Canvas, 44 × 51.5 cm
Inv.no. WRM1014. Given in 1898 by Frau
Peter Fuchs, Cologne

2

3

3
Juriaen van Streeck
Amsterdam 1632 – 1687 Amsterdam
Still life, after 1653
Oak, 54.5 × 44 cm
Inv.no. WRM2899. Given in 1954 by Otto
Wolff AG, Cologne, in memory of Herr
Dr Hans Hehemann
This small painting by the Amsterdam
artist is one of the finest still lifes in the
museum. Against a dark background,
illuminated by an invisible source,
precious objects decoratively arranged
form a still life that is particularly
effective in its subdued colour tones and
juxtaposition of textures. In the choice
of objects and of a dark background
Streeck follows Willem Kalf, but this
painting is an original masterpiece.

1

1
**Jan Hackaert and Adriaen van de
Velde**
**Amsterdam 1628/29 – c1685
Amsterdam; Amsterdam 1636 – 1672
Amsterdam**
River scene, c1660
Oak, 42.7 × 54.3 cm
Inv.no. WRM2557. Acquired in 1936 with
the Carstanjen collection

2
Frederick de Moucheron
Emden 1633 – 1686 Amsterdam
Mountain scene with herd of cattle
Canvas, 90.5 × 87 cm
Inv.no. WRM2561. Acquired in 1936 with
the Carstanjen collection

2

3

3
Jan Vermeer van Haarlem II
Haarlem 1628 – 1691 Haarlem
View of Haarlem, c1660-70
Oak, 42.5 × 78 cm
Inv.no. WRM2367. Given in 1928 by Herr
Julius Böhler, Munich

4
Ludolf Backhuysen
Emden 1631 – 1708 Amsterdam
Ships on the Zuiderzee before the Fort of
Naarden, c1660-70
Oak, 37.5 × 48.4 cm
Inv.no. WRM2566. Acquired in 1936 with
the Carstanjen collection

4

1

Jakob van Ruysdael
Haarlem 1628/29 – 1682 Amsterdam
Waterfall by a church, c1667-70
Canvas, 109 × 131.5 cm
Inv.no.2537. Acquired in 1936 with the
Carstanjen collection
Ruysdael often chose waterfalls as a
subject for his landscape paintings after
the 1650s, inspired by the dramatic
Scandinavian waterfall scenes of Allart
van Everdingen. Ruysdael's paintings
were done in Amsterdam, which
succeeded Haarlem as the centre of
landscape painting after the middle of
the century. At the same time a
heightened expression became
fashionable.

2

Jan Steen
Leyden 1625/26 – 1679 Leyden
Samson and Delilah, c1667-70
Canvas, 134 × 199 cm
Inv.no. WRM1024. Acquired in 1894
This splendid, large-scale painting shows
a typical Dutch combination of biblical
or mythological history painting with
the characteristics of narrative genre
painting. It depicts a scene from
Abraham Koninck's 1618 play, *The
Tragedy of Samson*, a parable of false
love.

1

2

3

Pieter de Hooch
Rotterdam 1629 – after 1684
Amsterdam
A couple with a parrot, c1675-80
Canvas, 73 × 62 cm
Inv.no. WRM3218. Acquired in 1968,
previously on loan from the Curators

and the Fördergesellschaft of the
Wallraf-Richartz Museum e.V.
Pieter de Hooch's painting belongs to
the 'haute-bourgeois' genre. Through an
anteroom we see a tidy living room with
an elegantly clothed couple. The man is
opening the cage with the parrot and the
woman is enticing the bird out with a

wine glass. These are clearly erotic
symbols which indicate that the young
woman is about to be seduced into an
affair.

3

1

Emanuel de Witte
Alkmaar c1617 – 1692 Amsterdam
Interior of a church, 1674
Canvas, 79 × 69 cm
Inv.no. WRM2620. Acquired in 1940

2

Abraham Mignon
Frankfurt am Main 1640 – 1679
Wetzlar or Utrecht
Still life, after 1672?
Canvas, 92 × 72.7 cm
Inv.no. WRM2838. Bequeathed in 1946 by
Herr Werner and Frau Juliane Lindgens,
Cologne

3

Gerhard ter Borch the Younger
Zwolle 1617 – 1681 Deventer
Portrait of a young man, c1670
Canvas, 46 × 37 cm
Inv.no. WRM1012. Acquired in 1886

4

Pieter van der Werff
Kralingen-Ambacht/Rotterdam 1665
– 1722 Rotterdam
Granida and Diafilo, 1711
Panel, 37 × 29 cm
Inv.no. Dep.478. On permanent loan
since 1984 from the Rudolf
Sieversleben'schen Otto Wolf Stiftung,
Cologne

5

Jacob van der Ulft
Gorinchem 1627 – 1689 Nordwijk
*Antique forum with a triumphal
procession*, c1670-79
Oak, 39.5 × 61.3 cm
Inv.no. WRM1062. Given in 1898 by Frau
Peter Fuchs, Cologne

1

2

3

4

5

Italian, French and Spanish painting from the sixteenth to eighteenth centuries

The painting of Italy, France and Spain including the Baroque period has never been a strong point in the Museum's collections. They include only a small number of pictures, which are insufficient to demonstrate general trends but can perhaps illuminate some important artists by representative works. Apart from Mattia Preti's *Judith with the head of Holofernes* and a few other works, the modern Italian gallery consists mainly of Venetian painting. The starting point is Paris Bordone's major work, *Bathsheba bathing*, painted in 1545, which has been in the possession of the Museum since 1870. Jacopo Tintoretto, like Bordone a pupil of Titian, and using colour in a closely related fashion, is represented in the collection by *The Entombment of Christ*. Tintoretto carried out many commissions for Venetian churches and civic buildings and essentially defined Venetian painting in the second half of the sixteenth century.

Earlier Venice had had to compete artistically with other cities, but in the eighteenth century the Venetian school became dominant in Italy. Giovanni Battista Tiepolo belongs to this period, as well as Francesco Guardi, Giovanni Battista Piazzetta, and the view-painter Antonio Canal, known as Canaletto, with his nephew Bernardo Bellotto.

Although it had a long tradition, view-painting reached its height during this period and Venice, with its special appeal for visitors to Italy, offered the *vedutisti* not only the subject matter but also the market for their paintings. Canaletto's *Grand Canal* so accurately depicts the scene that it can be dated to 1741-43 by the construction dates of the palazzi. He specialized in these views of Venice and, like Bellotto, was a highly prized artist abroad and was richly rewarded with commissions.

Giovanni Battista Piazzetta's *Country walk* was produced at about the same time as Canaletto's *Grand Canal*. Genre painting was his main area of activity, besides religious works. For Piazzetta, the depiction of the human figure was of central interest. He studied in Bologna with Giuseppe Maria Crespi but spent all his working life in Venice. He is well known for the strong contrasts of light and the drama of his compositions.

French painting of the seventeenth and eighteenth centuries in the Wallraf-Richartz Museum is represented by four great names, Claude Lorrain, Mathieu Le Nain, Hyacinthe Rigaud and François Boucher. Claude Lorrain's historical landscapes were a decisive influence on the development of European landscape painting, well into the nineteenth century. His *Harbour scene with grieving Heliades*, and particularly his *Landscape with the rescue of Psyche* are typical of Claude's vision of a landscape shaped by classical mythology, a landscape recognizable by its ancient monuments, which symbolize classical ideals.

French genre painting of the seventeenth century is represented in the collection by Mathieu Le Nain's *Gardener*. The three Le Nain brothers were specialists in genre and appear to have studied with a Flemish artist, at a time when genre painting was at its zenith in the Netherlands. Portraits were a requirement at court and demand flourished. Hyacinthe Rigaud, a pupil of Charles Lebrun and court painter to Louis XIV and Louis XV, was one of the most distinguished portraitists in Paris. He specialized in grand state portraits, but he also painted private portraits for wealthy citizens, such as *Everhard Jabach*, which shows the wealthy art collector and banker in informal house clothes.

A high point of mid-eighteenth-century French painting, which was very rich in talent, was the work of François Boucher, unmatched in his depiction of the brilliance of court life at the end of the Age of Absolutism. His small painting in the Museum of 1751 shows Louise O'Murphy, the mistress of Louis XV. Although Boucher produced more significant compositions, the identity of the model gives this painting historical as well as artistic interest.

Spanish painting is the smallest section in the gallery. There are only eight works, most dating from the seventeenth century, a period which was very productive for Spanish painting. Spain's extensive trade links brought with them an interchange of artistic ideas, particularly with Italy. Jusepe de Ribera played an important role in this. He began his studies with Ribalta but left Spain early on and went to Italy, where he discovered the work of Caravaggio. His style is characterized by strong light and shade, together with a realistic portrayal even of religious themes, as seen in his *St Paul the Hermit* of 1647.

Bartolomé Estéban Murillo was one of the most popular painters of the period and is still popular today, more for his genre paintings than his religious works. In 1898 the Museum purchased the large altarpiece *of St Francis in the chapel at Portiuncula, and* in 1936 two more works by Murillo came to the Museum with the Carstanjen collection, a *Penitent Mary Magdalene* and the genre *Old woman and boy*. This last painting shows an old woman trying to hide her plateful of broth from a street urchin. It is a typical Murillo genre scene, illustrating why he was so popular: he depicts poverty without suffering in a humane and humorous setting.

1

Paris Bordone
Treviso 1500 – 1571 Venice
Bathsheba bathing, c1545
Canvas, 234 × 217 cm
Inv.no. WRM517. Acquired in 1870

Organized around a strict central perspective, the painting has as its theme the guilty affair of king David. This moralizing subject was often painted because it justified portraying a nude.

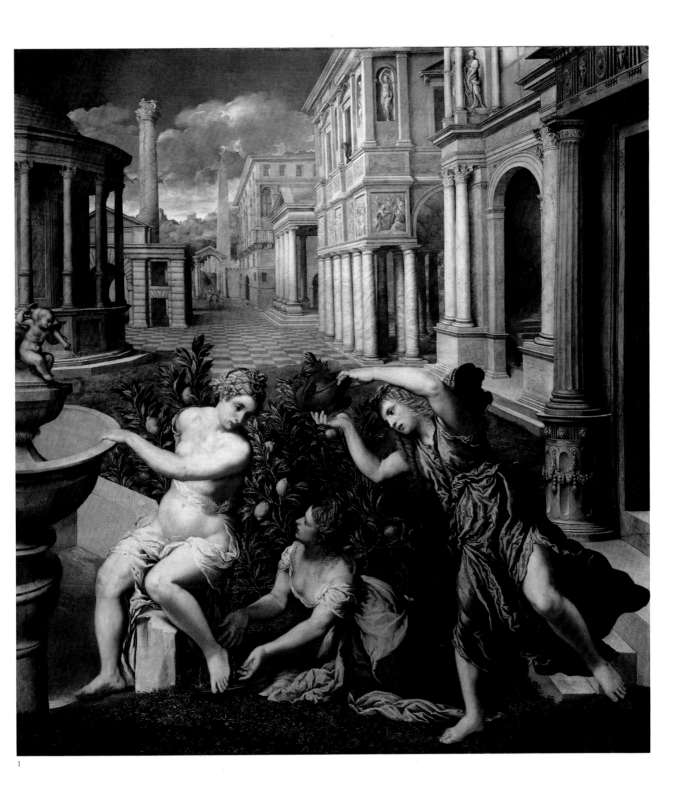

1

1

1
Antonio Canaletto
Venice 1697 – 1768 Venice
The Grand Canal in Venice, view to the
north from near the Rialto bridge, c1741-43
Canvas, 73 × 129 cm
Inv.no. WRM2549. Acquired in 1936 with
the Carstanjen collection

2

2

Jacopo Tintoretto
Venice 1518 – 1594 Venice
The Entombment of Christ, c1560
Canvas, 137 × 206 cm
Inv.no. Dep.277. On loan since 1966
from the German government
Crowded with figures and with great
movement, this painting not only
represents Christ's burial but also, by
the use of evocative motifs, recalls the
Descent from the Cross. The painting
illustrates Tintoretto's inventiveness and
his determination to convey the
emotional values of the biblical story.

3

Giovanni Battista Piazzetta
Venice 1682 – 1754 Venice
The country walk (Beach idyll), c1741-45
Canvas, 196.5 × 146 cm
Inv.no. WRM2806. Acquired in 1949

3

1

1
Claude Lorrain
Chamagne 1600 – 1682 Rome
Landscape with the rescue of Psyche
Canvas, 92 × 156.5 cm
Inv.no. WRM1050. Acquired in 1892

2
Hyacinthe Rigaud
Perpignan 1659 – 1743 Paris
Everhard Jabach, 1688
Canvas, 58.5 × 47 cm
Inv.no. WRM1066. Given in 1860 by Herr
Eduard Schenk, Cologne

2

3

4

3
Claude Lorrain
Chamagne 1600 – 1682 Rome
Harbour scene with grieving Heliades,
c1640
Canvas, 125.5 × 175.5 cm
Inv.no. WRM2646. Acquired in 1941

4
François Boucher
Paris 1703 – 1770 Paris
Girl reclining (Louise O'Murphy), 1751
Canvas, 59.5 × 73.5 cm
Inv.no. WRM2639. Acquired in 1941

Bartolomé Estéban Murillo
Seville 1618 – 1682 Seville
Old woman and boy, c1650-60
Canvas, 146 × 106 cm
Inv.no. WRM2541. Acquired in 1936 with
the Carstanjen collection

1

Jusepe de Ribera
Jativa 1591 – 1652 Naples
St Paul the Hermit, 1647
Canvas, 130 × 103.5 cm
Inv.no. WRM2553. Acquired in 1936 with
the Carstanjen collection

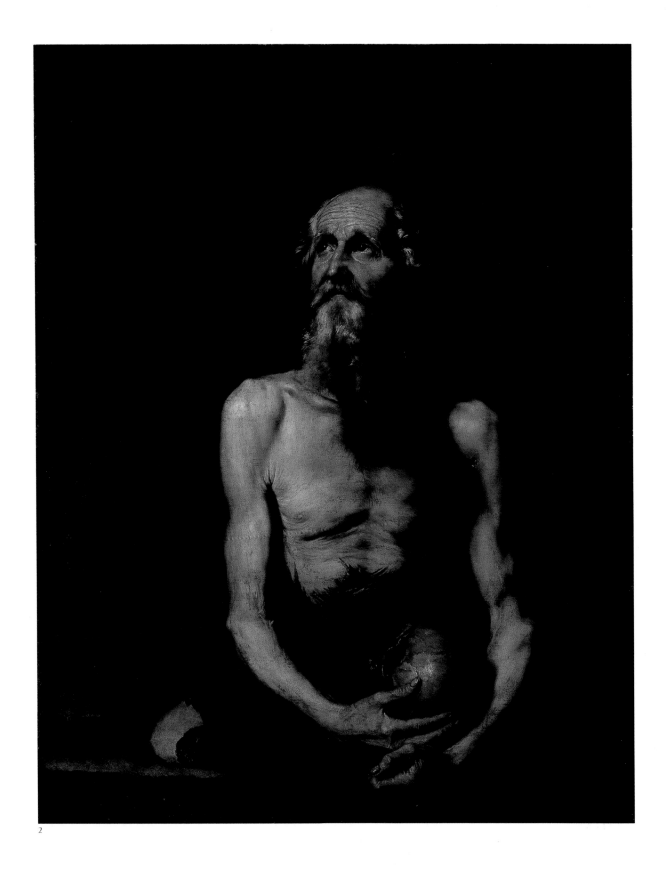

Jusepe de Ribera
Jativa 1591 – 1652 Naples
St Paul the Hermit, 1647
Canvas, 130 × 103.5 cm
Inv.no. WRM2553. Acquired in 1936 with
the Carstanjen collection

German painting in the nineteenth century

Nineteenth-century German painting has been collected by the Museum ever since its foundation. Although his main interests were historical and antiquarian, Franz Ferdinand Wallraf also owned works by contemporary artists. Until the appointment of Carl Aldenhoven in 1890, the Museum's directors were themselves artists, who had an open minded attitude to the work of their contemporaries and even left behind a few works of their own. However, avantgarde art only appeared in the Museum after the turn of the century and academic and history painting far outweighed it. Many of these academic paintings, which later fell out of favour, were sold in the 1930s and 1940s, while some, especially large works, were destroyed with the Museum building in 1943. Thus the emphasis in the collection of nineteenth-century German painting is not now on academic figurative painting but on Realist and Impressionist painting of the turn of the century (Wilhelm Leibl, Max Liebermann, Lovis Corinth) and the art of the Nazarenes and Romantics.

A group of German painters based in Rome in the early nineteenth century had a most decisive effect on the development of German art. The foremost of these artists was Joseph Anton Koch. He was born in Obergiblen in the Tyrol in 1768 but lived in Rome from spring 1795 to his death in 1839. Here he painted the 'heroic landscapes' which form the major part of his work. His *Mountain scene* of 1796, one of his earliest paintings, shows his attempt to continue the tradition of seventeenth-century landscape painting and to relate the heroic grandeur of nature to the human life that is dependent on it.

Carl Rottmann, who was a generation younger than Koch and also a specialist in landscape, was also drawn to the South. Although he did not settle there, he studied the scenery of Italy and Greece on extended visits. He produced in 1830, as a study for a fresco of the Arcadian Fields in the Hofgarten in Munich, the Museum's view of the rock of Cefalù in northern Sicily. In contrast to Koch, Rottmann's paintings are topographical. He wanted to depict accurately an existing geographical situation. Equally important to him was the place's historical significance.

The experience of Italy was not only decisive for the majority of German landscape artists of the nineteenth century but also for figurative painting, secular as well as sacred. In 1818 Julius Schnorr von Carolsfeld moved to Rome from his home town of Leipzig. There he joined the Lukas-Bund (Guild of St Luke), an artists' group originally set up by Friedrich Overbeck and Franz Pforr in Vienna in opposition to the academy there. After Overbeck and Pforr had moved to Rome the Lukas-Bund exercised great influence (though Pforr died in 1812), and not only on the German artists in Rome. The members of the group, called the 'Nazarenes' after their long hair like Christ's, wanted to return to what they saw as the simple truth and piety of Dürer and the early Italian Renaissance. They tried in their work to employ the forms, style and colour of the Old Masters. Schnorr's *Madonna and Child*, painted in Rome in 1820, has been in the Museum since 1885. The composition and clear luminous colour of the work illustrates Schnorr's intensive, creative relationship with the Italian Renaissance.

While the majority of German artists lived in Rome, particularly in the early nineteenth century, or undertook extended visits to Italy, a few still managed to resist the pull of the South. One of these was Caspar David Friedrich, who studied in northern Germany and Denmark, and then, apart from a few trips within Germany and Bohemia, chose to settle in Dresden and never left it. Friedrich dedicated himself almost exclusively to painting landscapes, but his main objective was not the depiction of natural phenomena. The exact observation of nature was merely the basis for his symbolic content, which used the medium of landscape to contemplate the human condition and man's relationship with nature and with God. Friedrich's small painting, *Oak in the snow*, acquired in 1942, is based on accurate observation, and yet the image of the gnarled oak tree also has symbolic significance.

Adolf von Menzel's *Storm on Tempelhof mountain* was painted only six years after the death of Caspar David Friedrich. This small-format picture is an example of a completely different conception of the role of landscape painting. Menzel's art is significant for its break with the German tradition of landscape painting. With Blechen, Menzel was a pioneer of realistic landscape, landscape with no symbolic content or didactic purpose, of which the composition and colour adhere strictly to nature.

In the second half of the century, realism increased in German painting. The later 'Roman' Germans, especially Feuerbach, Böcklin and Marées, and lastly the much younger Max Klinger, tried to counter this trend with their huge compositions on traditional themes from classical mythology, history and literature, but their idealistic view of art did not prevail. Although the classical figurative composition was held up as the model in the academies, from the late 1860s the majority of artists were more interested in the themes and techniques of realism.

One of the main exponents of the anti-academic movement was Wilhelm Leibl. Born in Cologne in 1844, he studied at the Munich Academy and, after his studies and a short spell in Paris, lived and worked in various villages in Upper Bavaria in complete withdrawal from society. In 1869, when still a student, he had his first experience of contemporary French art. The work of Gustave Courbet, in particular, made a great impression upon him and showed him the way to develop his own ideas. Leibl was primarily preoccupied with the portrayal of the people where he lived. He always painted from a model, and would not work from memory in case he should not achieve an accurate representation. Since 1911, with the purchase of the collection of the Berlin Kommerzienrat Ernst Seeger, the Wallraf-Richartz Museum has possessed a very large collection of Leibl's work.

Max Liebermann was also concerned with the problems of realism in painting. He was not primarily a portraitist but his greatest achievement was in the depiction of groups of figures. His subjects were working people, and later people at leisure, out in the open.

Like Liebermann, Lovis Corinth began with figural compositions in a realistic, unbeautified manner. After the turn of the century, his palette became brighter and he eventually developed a style in which forms are increasingly blurred in gradations of colour. In this he is more daring and modern than Liebermann. Corinth was interested in all genres of painting, from still life to landscapes, from portraits to mythological and religious themes. The paintings by Corinth in the Museum show the whole range of his work and form a bridge to the styles and trends of later twentieth-century German painting on display in the Ludwig Museum.

1

1
Jacob Philipp Hackert
Prenzlau 1731 – 1807 San Piero di Careggio
Autumn: grape harvest and view of Sorrento, the Gulf of Naples and the islands, c1784
Oil on canvas, 96.5 × 64 cm
Inv.no. WRM25117. Acquired with funds from the De Noël Trust

1

Joseph Anton Koch
Obergiblen 1768 – 1839 Rome
Mountain scene, 1796
Oil on canvas, 110 × 161.5 cm
Inv.no. WRM2601. Acquired in 1937

2

Carl Rottmann
Handschuhsheim 1798 – 1850
Munich
Cefalù, 1830
Oil on canvas, 63 × 79 cm
Inv.no. WRM1107. Acquired with funds
from the Richartz Trust

3

4

5

3
Ferdinand Georg Waldmüller
Vienna 1793 – 1865 Vienna
The birthday table, 1840
Oil on oak panel, 63 × 50 cm
Inv.no. WRM2593. Acquired in 1937

4
Carl Begas the Elder
Heinsberg/Aachen 1794 – 1854
Berlin
The Begas family, 1821
Oil on canvas, 76 × 85.5 cm
Inv.no. WRM1556. Given by the Begas
family

5
Karl Eduard Ferdinand Blechen
Cottbus 1798 – 1840 Berlin
Grotto in the Gulf of Naples, 1829
Oil on oak panel, 37.5 × 29 cm
Inv.no. WRM2603. Acquired in 1938

1
Julius Schnorr von Carolsfeld
Leipzig 1794 – 1872 Dresden
Madonna and Child, 1820
Oil on canvas, 74 × 62 cm
Inv.no. WRM1112. Acquired in 1885

2
Caspar David Friedrich
Greifswald 1774 – 1840 Dresden
Oak in the snow
Oil on canvas, 44 × 34.5 cm
Inv.no. WRM2666. Acquired in 1942

The oak is a symbol of the pre-Christian world. The fallen branches denote the meaninglessness of heathen existence, while signs of spring in the melting snow and the blue sky herald new life in Christ.

1

2

1

1

Arnold Böcklin
Basel 1827 – 1901 Florence
Attack by pirates
Colour varnish on mahogany panel,
153 × 232 cm
Inv.no. WRM1143. Given in 1904 by the
Cologne Friends of Art

2

Hans von Marées
Elberfeld 1837 – 1847 Rome
Eclogue
Oil on canvas, 100 × 75 cm
Inv.no. WRM2412. Acquired with support
from Herrs Heinrich and Hermann
Neuerburg and Herr Richard von
Schnitzler

3

Anselm Friedrich Feuerbach
Speyer 1829 – 1880 Venice
Nanna, c1861
Oil on canvas, 73.5 × 55.5 cm
Inv.no. WRM2372. Acquired in 1929
From 1860 to 1865 Anna Risi, a cobbler
from Trastevere in Rome, was Anselm
Feuerbach's model. He believed that in
her he had found the embodiment of
classical ideals of beauty and so she sat
for him for a series of mythological,
religious and literary subjects. The real
model was essential to Feuerbach
despite the idealism of his sketches.

4

Adolf Friedrich Erdmann von
Menzel
Breslau 1815 – 1905 Berlin
Storm on Tempelhof mountain, 1846
Oil on paper on board, 31 × 47 cm
Inv.no. WRM1126. Given by the Society of
Friends of the Museum

2

3

4

1

Wilhelm Leibl
Cologne 1844 – 1900 Würzburg
Old Parisian woman
Oil on mahogany panel, 81.5 × 64.5 cm
Inv.no. WRM1169. Acquired in 1911

1

2

Wilhelm Leibl
Cologne 1844 – 1900 Würzburg
Young Parisian woman, 1869
Oil on mahogany panel, 64.5 × 52.5 cm
Inv.no. WRM1170. Acquired in 1911

Like the *Old Parisian woman*, this
picture dates from Leibl's visit to Paris
in 1869-70. For some years it was in the
possession of the American painter
William Merrit Chase and demonstrates
Leibl's familiarity with the current Paris
art scene.

2

1

2

3

1
Wilhelm Leibl
Cologne 1844 – 1900 Würzburg
The corset (fragment)
Oil on mahogany panel, 27 × 21.5 cm
Inv.no. WRM1177. Given in 1911 by Herr
Alfred Schütte, Cologne
This example of Leibl's minute and exact
technique (almost like Holbein's) enjoys
great popularity. The little mahogany
panel is a fragment of a painting, *Girl
with carnation*, which Leibl cut up
because he was not satisfied with the
painting as a whole. However, it is
complete in itself.

2
Wilhelm Leibl
Cologne 1844 – 1900 Würzburg
Girl at the window, 1899
Oil on canvas, 109 × 72.5 cm
Inv.no. WRM1161. Acquired in 1911
This painting is one of the artist's last
works. It shows Leibl at the zenith of his
powers. Leibl believed that the figure
was the most worthy expression of
nature, of which his work was an
attempt to grasp the essence.

3
Max Liebermann
Berlin 1847 – 1935 Berlin
Bleaching linen on the grass, 1882
Oil on canvas, 109 × 173 cm
Inv.no. WRM2939. Acquired in 1954
This picture with its homely subject
exudes an almost spiritual sense of
peace in the old orchard. Originally
there was a third washerwoman in the
foreground on the right near the
washtub, which dominated the
composition. Liebermann painted over
the figure after the painting came back
from exhibition in the Paris Salon of
1883.

4
Max Liebermann
Berlin 1847 – 1935 Berlin
Judengasse in Amsterdam, 1905
Oil on canvas, 59 × 73 cm
Inv.no. WRM1189. Given in 1909 by Herr
Louis Hagen, Cologne

5
Max Liebermann
Berlin 1847 – 1935 Berlin
Horse and groom, 1912
Oil on board, nailed to a wedge-shaped
frame, 81 × 64.5 cm
Inv.no. WRM1190. Acquired in 1913 with
funds from the Joann Nepomuk
Heidemann Trust through the
Fördergesellschaft des Wallraf-Richartz-
Museums

4

5

1

2

1
Lovis Corinth
Tapiau 1858 – 1925 Zandvoort
Kaiser Day in Hamburg, 1911
Oil on canvas, 70.5 × 90.5 cm
Inv.no. WRM2585. Acquired in 1936

2
Lovis Corinth
Tapiau 1858 – 1925 Zandvoort
Panorama of Walchensee (Walchensee,
view from the Cockpit), 1924
Oil on canvas, 101 × 200 cm
Inv.no. WRM2886. Acquired in 1952 with
support from Bayer AG, Leverkusen

3

3
Lovis Corinth
Tapiau 1858 – 1925 Zandvoort
Self-portrait in white smock, 1912
Oil on canvas, 101 × 200 cm
Inv.no. WRM2368. Acquired in 1928 with
support from Galerie Matthiesen, Berlin

1

1
Christian Rohlfs
Niendorff bei Segeberg 1849 – 1938
Hagen
Forest path in winter (Chaussée to
Tiefurt, Webicht near Weimar)
Oil on canvas, 59.5 × 74.5 cm
Inv.no. WRM2460. Acquired in 1934

2
Max Slevogt
Landshut 1868 – 1932 Neukastel
Cherry harvest: view from Neukastel
looking south, 1926
Oil on canvas, 90.5 × 116 cm
Inv.no. WRM2361. Acquired in 1928 with
support from Herr Hackenbroich,
Frankfurt am Main

3
Max Slevogt
Landshut 1868 – 1932 Neukastel
Vine pergola, Neukastel, 1917
Oil on limewood panel, 61 × 49.5 cm
Inv.no. WRM2596. Acquired in 1937

2

3

French painting in the nineteenth century

Nineteenth-century French painting forms an important part of the collection of the Wallraf-Richartz Museum. The overwhelming significance of French painting for the development of art, including German art, led even before the First World War to the purchase of paintings which still today determine the profile of the museum. Even then most of the pictures bought were from the second half of the nineteenth century. Works by Courbet, Renoir, van Gogh and Gauguin found their way into the collection under the progressive directorship of Alfred Hagelstange until 1914, the year of his death. In the 1960s the French section was enhanced by the acquisition of a series of Impressionist paintings. This included works by Sisley and Monet as well as pictures by Manet and Cézanne. Although the collection of nineteenth-century French art may not be very extensive, it nevertheless offers a good overview of key developments as well as insights into the work of the most important artists.

In 1855 Gustave Courbet organized an exhibition in Paris entirely of his own paintings which he called *Le Réalisme*. This title defined not only Courbet's artistic conviction but gave a name to a new style. For Courbet, only what was empirically there could be represented, and then only in the form and the colour of the original subject. This approach was in conflict with the then current doctrine of art, the Academy and also the views of the majority of artists. His large painting *The hunt breakfast* of 1858, acquired in 1910, is an impressive example of his approach, an everyday scene rendered exactly in ordinary, subdued colours.

Courbet had no pupils and yet his influence on French painting can hardly be overestimated. The Impressionists looked back both to him and to the Barbizon painters, particularly Auguste Renoir, who at the beginning of his career studied Courbet's works in the 1860s and found much for his own use in them. One of the main works from his early career is '*Mr and Mrs Alfred Sisley*' of 1868, which has been in the Museum since 1912.

Pissarro was also influenced by the Barbizon painters. From the 1860s he worked with Renoir and Claude Monet and was also very important for the development of Impressionist landscape painting. His large picture *L'Hermitage near Pontoise* dates from shortly before Renoir's portrait of the Sisleys and, like it, uses subdued colours. Corot's open air painting, with its restrained and differentiated colour values and his attempt to capture momentary impressions of landscape, were as influential for Pissarro as Courbet's realistic representation of landscape forms in broad, rapid brushstrokes.

While there is a definite heaviness like that of realist painting in Pissarro's *L'Hermitage near Pontoise*, Alfred Sisley's *Bridge at Hampton Court* is a completely Impressionistic landscape dating from 1874, the year of the first Impressionist group exhibition. Although Sisley is not one of the main initiators of the Impressionist movement, nevertheless in his own field, landscape painting, he produced pictures which in their spontaneity, atmospheric effect, colour and facture are some of the most significant works of French Impressionism.

Though he can not be counted as one of the Impressionist group, nor did he take part in any of their exhibitions, Edouard Manet moved in the same circles as these painters. His artistic development had different beginnings. As a pupil of Thomas Couture, himself a pupil of Eugène Delacroix, he was firmly in the tradition of academic history painting. After this came a meticulous study of the great works of earlier artists, particularly Spanish painting. Manet was almost exclusively occupied with figural compositions and painted very few landscapes. However, from 1880 to his early death in 1883 he worked intensively on the still life, with the aim of adding new creations of the highest quality to this much neglected genre. His *Bundle of asparagus* from 1880 – originally owned by Max Liebermann and in the Museum since 1968 – is characterized, like his other still lifes, by the great simplicity of its composition. For Manet the interest of the object lay not in its value, meaning or rarity – as in earlier still life painting – but in its appearance, colour and form, and in this Manet was an Impressionist.

Claude Monet, however, was the first to concern himself with the problems of Impressionism and, in the area of landscape painting, contributed most to its development. The Museum possesses a view by him of the Seine and *Fishing boats on the beach at Étretat*, a painting of the mid-1880s. Near the end of the 1880s, Monet began to lay out a huge garden with Japanese ornamental ponds at Giverny, a village on the Seine near Vernon. In following years he was preoccupied with large canvases and more and more exclusively with motifs from the garden. These included a series of paintings of the lilypond, the Japanese bridge, flower borders and the rose pergola. In 1914-17 Monet painted the big *Waterlilies* in the Museum which embodies his late style.

Impressionism was only one of the range of artistic forms in French painting of the late nineteenth century. Many artists produced Impressionist works only for a limited period in their career. One example is Paul Cézanne, who, in the 1870s, followed Impressionist principles under the influence of Pissarro. However, he soon developed a way of painting in brushstrokes like cubes and bars in order to analyse form and perspective. Other artists, such as Odilon Redon, were never concerned with the realities of their surroundings. Redon, born in the same year as Monet, lived in his own imaginative world. He was associated with the Nabis, a group of painters, including Gauguin, Bonnard and Vuillard, who sought to express their feelings about the world in images symbolic rather than realist. These painters, too, are represented in the Museum by individual works.

1

1
Jean Baptiste Camille Corot
Paris 1796 – 1875 Paris
Poetry
Oil on canvas, 55 × 45.5 cm
Inv.no. WRM2651. Acquired in 1941

1

Gustave Courbet
Ornans 1819 – 1877 La Tour de Peilz
The hunt breakfast, 1858
Oil on canvas, 207 × 325 cm
Inv.no. WRM1171. Given in 1910 by Herr
Leonard Tietz, Cologne

2

Gustave Courbet
Ornans 1819 – 1877 La Tour de Peilz
Beach near Trouville, 1865
Oil on canvas, 53.5 × 64 cm
Inv.no. WRM2905. Given in 1956 by the
Gutehoffnungshütte, Oberhausen
This picture, painted by Courbet in the
bathing resort of Trouville,
provocatively has no identifiable subject
and its effect lies entirely in the finely
differentiated grey, ochre and blue
colour tones which build up the image of
beach, sea and sky in horizontal parallel
bands.

2

3
Camille Pissarro
St Thomas (Antilles) 1830 – 1903
Paris
L'Hermitage near Pontoise, 1867
Oil on canvas, 91 × 150.5 cm
Inv.no. WRM3119. Acquired in 1961

4
Alfred Sisley
Paris 1839 – 1899 Moret sur Loing
Bridge at Hampton Court, 1877
Oil on canvas, 45.5 × 61 cm
Inv.no. WRM2929. Acquired in 1956 from
the Rheinland and Westphalian Society
for the Arts, Düsseldorf
Sisley stayed near Hampton Court from
July to October 1874 and painted some

of his best landscape pictures there. The
conveyance of movement here is one of
his main concerns, illustrating one of
Sisley's fundamental principles that the
most important and most difficult part of
painting was to give life to the image.

3

4

1
Gustave Caillebotte
Paris 1848 – 1894 Gennevilliers
Washing drying on the banks of the Seine
Oil on canvas, 106 × 150 cm
Inv.no. Dep. 447. On loan from the
Board of Curators and the
Fördergesellschaft des Wallraf-Richartz
Museums/Ludwig Museums e.V.

2
Edouard Manet
Paris 1832 – 1883 Paris
Bundle of asparagus, 1880
Oil on canvas, 46 × 55 cm
Inv.no. Dep. 318. On loan since 1968
from the Society of Friends, the Board of
Curators and the Fördergesellschaft des
Wallraf-Richartz Museums e.V.

1

3
Auguste Renoir
Limoges 1841 – 1919 Cagnes
'Mr and Mrs Alfred Sisley', 1868
Oil on canvas, 105 × 75 cm
Inv.no. WRM1199. Acquired in 1912
This portrait of Alfred Sisley and his
companion (probably not his wife Marie,
as has been traditionally assumed, but
most likely Renoir's model, Lise Trehot),
is an early example of Impressionist
painting. Though still bound by colour
and form with realistic detail and
subdued light, nevertheless in the
portrayal of a transitory moment with a
scarcely discernible background of
bushes and borders it is already an
example of Impressionism by its choice
of subject and viewpoint.

2

1

2

1
Claude Monet
Paris 1840 – 1926 Giverny
View of the Seine
Oil on canvas, 67 × 82.5 cm
Inv.no. WRM2949. Given in 1954 by
Kaufhof AG, Cologne, on the seventy-
fifth anniversary of their founding

2
Claude Monet
Paris 1840 – 1926 Giverny
Fishing boats on the beach at Étretat,
Oil on canvas, 74 × 101 cm
Inv.no. WRM3120. Acquired in 1961

3
Paul Cézanne
Aix-en-Provence 1839 – 1906 Aix-en-
Provence
Landscape west of Aix-en-Provence,
1885-87
Oil on canvas, 65 × 81 cm
Inv.no. WRM3188. Acquired in 1965 with
the support of the Rheinland Friends of
Art, several Cologne firms and
Westdeutsche Rundfunk

4
Paul Cézanne
Aix-en-Provence 1839 – 1906 Aix-en-
Provence
Still life with pears
Oil on canvas, 38 × 46 cm
Inv.no. WRM3189. Acquired in 1965 with
the support of Rheinland Friends of Art,
several Cologne firms and Westdeutsche
Rundfunk

3

4

1
Paul Gauguin
Paris 1848 – 1903 La Dominique
(Marquesas Islands)
Breton youth, 1889
Oil on canvas, 93 × 73.5 cm
Inv.no. WRM3114. Acquired in 1961 with
support from Herr and Frau S. van
Deventer, De Steeg

2
Ferdinand Hodler
Gurzelen 1853 – 1918 Geneva
Study of the head of an Italian woman
(Giulia Leonardi), 1910?
Oil on canvas, 34.5 × 40 cm
Inv.no. WRM1210. Given by Herr Louis
Lehmann

3
Vincent van Gogh
Groot Zandert 1853 – 1890 Auvers-
sur-Oise
The lifting bridge, 1888
Oil on canvas, 49.5 × 64 cm
Inv.no. WRM1197. Acquired in 1911

4
Edouard Vuillard
Cuiseaux 1868 – 1940 La Baule
Girl at cupboard, c1895
Oil on board over wood, 37 × 33.5 cm
Inv.no. WRM3049. Acquired in 1958 with
the Strecker collection, Wiesbaden

5
Edouard Vuillard
Cuiseaux 1868 – 1940 La Baule
Woman in a studio
Tempera on paper over canvas,
85.5 × 94 cm
Inv.no. WRM3145. Acquired in 1961

1

2

3

4

5

1

2

1
Edgar Degas
Paris 1834 – 1917 Paris
Dancers, c1905
Pastels on paper over canvas,
45.6 × 93.7 cm
Inv.no. WRM3122. Acquired in 1961

2
Claude Monet
Paris 1840 – 1926 Giverny
Waterlilies (Nymphéas), 1913-17
Oil on canvas, 180 × 205 cm
Inv.no. WRM3266. Acquired with support
from the Land of Nordrhein-Westfalen,
the Board of Curators and the
Fördergesellschaft des Wallraf-Richartz
Museums/Ludwig Museums e.V.
In the course of Monet's artistic
development the subject became less
and less important. It was necessary as
the source of inspiration but
increasingly only served as the pretext
for the representation of colour
mutations. And so the actual waterlilies
are hardly discernible here, but have
become almost abstract. The only things
that Monet seems to be interested in are
the colours – they are transferred on to
the canvas at the moment of perception
and thus become the immediate
impression of the experience.

3
Odilon Redon
Bordeaux 1840 – 1916 Paris
St George and the dragon, c1900
Oil on poplar panel, 29.5 × 27 cm
Inv.no. WRM2812. Acquired in 1949 from
the Josef Haubrich collection

4
Pierre Bonnard
Fontenay-aux-Roses 1867 – 1947
Le Cannet
In the boat (Vernon),
Oil on canvas, 81.5 × 116 cm
Inv.no. WRM3238. Acquired in 1973 with
support from the Land of Nordrhein-
Westfalen, the Board of Curators and the
Fördergesellschaft des Wallraf-Richartz
Museums/Ludwig Museums e.V.

3

4

1

James Ensor
Ostende 1860 – 1949 Ostende
Skeleton watching chinoiserie
Oil on canvas, 99.5 × 64.5 cm
Inv.no. WRM2741. Given in 1946 by Dr
Josef Haubrich, Cologne

2

Pierre Bonnard
Fontenay-aux-Roses 1867 – 1947
Le Cannet
Nude in a mirror
Oil on canvas, 123 × 46 cm
Inv.no. Dep. 446. On loan from the
Board of Curators and the
Fördergesellschaft des Wallraf-Richartz
Museums/Ludwig Museums e. V.

1

2

Edvard Munch
Loeiten 1863 – 1944 Ekely
Four girls on a bridge, 1905
Oil on canvas, 126 × 126 cm
Inv.no. WRM2816. Given in 1949 by the
Cologne Friends of Art

3

Graphic Arts

A 'museum within a museum' – the collection of prints and drawings in the Wallraf-Richartz Museum, while an integral part of the Museum, is also a self-contained whole, rather like the cabinet of engravings of former times. The collection has two main origins: Franz Ferdinand Wallraf's collection of graphic works and the older collection from the Cologne Jesuit College. With numerous gifts and purchases over time, the collection has grown to be extensive and varied.

The most valuable items in the collection are undoubtedly the medieval miniatures (more than 200 items) and the drawings and watercolours (more than 8,000 items). The largest part of the collection consists of prints (more than 45,000). In addition there is a separate collection of approximately 8,000 items from the estate of the architect Jakob Ignaz Hittorff. Altogether these works range from the high Middle Ages to the beginning of the twentieth century. In the area of medieval book illumination, one work in particular stands out, the Book of Hours of Sophia von Bylant (c1475). It is decorated with miniatures by the Cologne Master of St Bartholomew and is one of the greatest examples of Late Gothic illuminated manuscripts. Also of great art-historical significance in this section are the miniature folios from the Cologne convent of the nuns of St Clare.

Drawings and watercolours are an important part of any collection of graphic art. The Museum's collection has a substantial number of works by the leading artists of the great epochs of art history. Drawings are fascinating works of art in their own right. A drawing expresses the individuality of the creative personality. The different drawing styles, like handwriting, show the way of seeing, the process of perception, the artistic temperament and the objectives of individual artists. The range of drawing techniques and media and their combination is almost limitless. The simplicity and clarity of the medium reveals the expression of creative power with great immediacy. Drawings are also informative about the conditions of artistic production. They can have the most varied functions, from a subordinate role in the creative process – as in medieval pattern books or preparatory studies for painting, sculpture or architecture – to works of art in their own right. A drawing takes us, in the words of Max Liebermann, not only into the artist's studio but also deep inside his personality.

The collection demonstrates the varied nature of drawing. A particularly good example is a valuable sheet of Leonardo da Vinci with figure studies for *The Adoration of the Magi* (c1481), on the back of which are two lively studies of crabs. This sheet shows his clear, structured drawing style and the classically inspired ideal forms of the Florentine Renaissance, as well as the precise observation of nature and the artist's wide-ranging interests. A lively sketch by Raphael and a sheet of studies by Andrea del Sarto are further examples from this important epoch. Many other Italian masters until the time of Giovanni Battista Tiepolo, Giovanni Battista Piazzetta and Francesco Guardi are also represented.

Besides these the group of German drawings is equally extensive and no less significant. Among works by the early German masters the most important must be three sheets by Albrecht Dürer, including a brush drawing of the *Virgin Mary with the Child in a niche* (1494 or 1495-96). There are also works by Hans Leonhard Schäufelein and Erhard Schön. From the German Baroque drawings by Paul Egell, Johann Heinrich Tischbein the Elder and Ignaz Günther are worthy of particular mention.

The third most important school is that of the Netherlands. Here there are drawings by Jan van Scorel, Esaias van de Velde and Jan van Goyen, which clearly show the development of new forms of landscape painting. Drawings by Rembrandt and his school are the most significant works in this section, of which in turn the most important is the splendid *Christ and the Woman taken in adultery* (c1659). It is a preparatory sketch, summarized with powerful characterization, which gives us insight into the complex process of working out the idea of a picture.

Only a few years ago attention turned once more to the section of French Baroque drawings. Since then several splendid drawings have come into the collection, including works by Hyacinthe Rigaud, Hubert Robert and Jean-Honoré Fragonard. In contrast to the lively variety of the extrovert Rococo style, the imagery of the German Romantics is stark and often inward looking. There are leaves from sketchbooks and fully worked-out drawings by Caspar David Friedrich as well as Philipp Otto Runge's finely wrought drawing of *Genii on a lily* (1809) which was a preparatory study for his painting *Morning*. In addition there are drawings by Julius Schnorr von Carolsfeld, Joseph Anton Koch and Johann Anton Ramboux, marking the transition to the plurality of styles typical of the nineteenth century. Prominent artists on the international

1

1
The Master of St Bartholomew
Active in Cologne c1480/85 – c1510
Crucifixion from the Book of Hours of
Sophia von Bylant, 1475
Opaque colour, gold leaf on parchment;
this folio 23.2 × 16.5 cm
Inv.no. 1961/32. Acquired with the
assistance of the German Government,
the Land of Nordrhein-Westfalen, the
Landschaftsverband and 132 industrial,
commercial, banking and insurance
companies
The Bylant Book of Hours shows the
magnificence and expressive
achievement of book illumination at its
zenith at the end of the Middle Ages.
The miniatures by the St Bartholomew
master in this codex are the earliest
identifiable works by this painter who
was a leading workshop master in the
late medieval Cologne school around
1500.

art scene in Europe at that time are also represented – Théodore
Géricault, Théodore Rousseau and Jean-François Millet.
Associated with them are works by German artists like Adolf von
Menzel, Wilhelm Leibl and Max Liebermann.

The remaining works form a fitting finale to the Museum's
collection, ending as it does at the beginning of the twentieth
century. Works by Auguste Rodin, Paul Signac and Edouard
Viullard lead us into the formal world of the turn of the century
and the beginning of the modern era. Their subjectivity of
perception and expressive use of colour, their flat surfaces and
tendency to abstraction herald the decisive developments of art in
the twentieth century.

After the drawings the prints may seem of secondary
importance, but that is to do them an injustice. Of course most
are not unique creations, but intended for multiple production.
However, the same power of composition, variety and
sophistication of techniques and range of effects are to be found.
Not even the briefest overview of the development from the
'incunabula' of the late Middle Ages to the artistic graphic works
of the turn of the century is possible here. However, it is worth
noting that when the collection of engravings was opened to the
public in Cologne just after 1900 it was the prints that attracted
the most interest. It was seen as having an important role as an
archive documenting the best in artistic developments.

The sensitivity to light of the works that are conserved in the
graphics collection makes it impossible to show its treasures on
open display. 'Art on paper' for most of the time has to be
protected in boxes and cupboards. However, they are not
completely inaccessible to the interested visitor. In the viewing
room, which is situated centrally by the main hall staircase in the
new building, works can be viewed at set times or by special
arrangement. Catalogues where available and the inventory index
make the collection accessible. Apart from this, special
exhibitions are held regularly, where a selection of works on a
particular theme is on public display. These exhibitions are held
in the purpose-built rooms close to the staircase on the same level
as the Wallraf-Richartz Museum, or in the large exhibition gallery.
The exhibition programme not only reflects the content of the
collection but also includes works loaned from other museums
and collections, to show the whole range and highest quality of
works from all areas of the graphic arts.

1
Leonardo da Vinci
Vinci near Empoli 1452 – 1519 Cloux near Amboise
Studies of crabs, c1481
Quill pen and ink, 27.3 × 17.6 cm
Inv.no. Z 2003 (verso), Old Collection
With brief pen strokes the form and life of the crabs are captured, poised to repel attack. With nature studies, drawing in the Renaissance becomes a document of a new world view – a form of artistic 'research and development' in its own right.

2
Albrecht Dürer
Nuremberg 1471 – 1528 Nuremberg
The Virgin Mary with the Child in a niche, c1494-96
Brush, 21.8 × 17.1 cm
Inv.no. Z 130, Old Collection
This early Madonna with its lithe forms and soft light-dark transitions is still very much in the Late Gothic style. Dürer here may be inspired by sculptural models which he saw during his stay in the Upper Rhine area.

3
Rembrandt van Rijn
Leyden 1606 – 1669 Amsterdam
Christ and the Woman taken in adultery, c1659
Reed pen and brush, 9.9 × 16.4 cm
Inv.no. Z 1786, Old Collection
This study shows Rembrandt's mature mastery of his media. The idea of the picture evolves spontaneously and dynamically during the process of drawing, as can be seen from the corrections and in the addition of a strip of paper on the right-hand side of the page.

4
Hyacinthe Rigaud
Perpignan 1659 – 1743 Paris
Studies for a self-portrait, probably 1730
Chalk, 27.8 × 45.4 cm
Inv.no. 1961/26. Given by Herr and Frau Manfred Dunkel, Cologne
Rigaud's fascinating and beautiful study is executed using a sophisticated technique: black and white chalk strokes on coloured paper create an unprecedented sculptural effect. The subject – the painter himself – is dissected in detail.

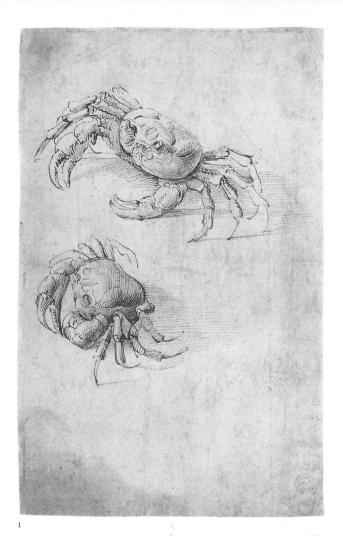

1

2

3

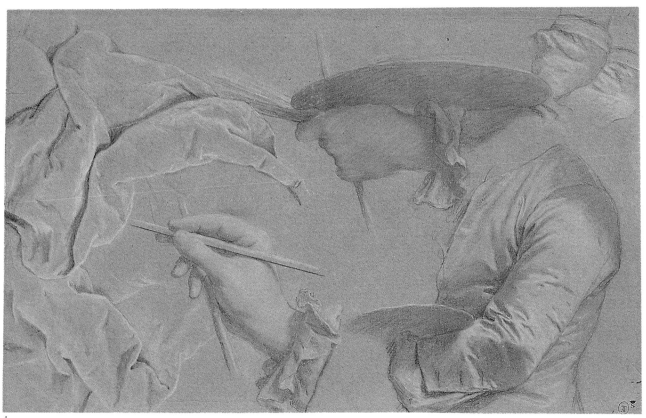

4

1
Franz Ignaz Günter
Altmannstein 1725 – 1775 Munich
The Muse Clio writing history, c1763
Brush, 31.8 × 18.2 cm
Inv.no. Z 1104, Old Collection
This is a study for an allegorical title
page of a book, in which Clio, the Muse
of History, is accompanied by Chronos
(Time) and Fame.

2
Johann Anton de Peters
Cologne 1725 – 1795 Cologne
The happy mother, c1775
Watercolour, 57.3 × 42 cm
Inv.no. Z 1043, Old Collection. Wallraf
collection (1791)
The creator of this charming watercolour
was born in Cologne and became famous
in Paris. Franz Ferdinand Wallraf
acquired a part of his estate.

3

Jean-Honoré Fragonard
Grasse 1732 – 1806 Paris
The pretty cook, c1775
Red chalk, 33.5 × 24.6 cm
Inv.no. 1944/6. Acquired in 1944

This kitchen scene, an everyday subject, seems to be lit up by the elegant clarity of the line. Fragonard's drawing style has the spirit of Rococo and yet there is also an element of Roman classicism. The clarity of the hatching is remarkable.

3

123

1
Johann Anton Ramboux
Trier 1790 – 1866 Cologne
Opening from the artist's Italian and
German sketchbook
Pencil, double page, 12.9 × 16.3 cm
Inv.no. 1936/23 (ZB 10). Acquired in 1936
Ramboux, who from 1844 was curator of
the Wallraf-Richartz Museum, studied
under Jacques-Louis David in Paris in his
youth. He drew the sights of his many
travels in extensive sketchbooks.

2
Jakob Ignaz Hittorff
Cologne 1792 – 1867 Paris
*Reconstruction of the Temple of Hercules
at Cori*, after 1822
Pen and wash over pencil, 61.3 × 48.9 cm
Inv.no. Ital.196, Hittorff estate (1899)
Originally from Cologne, Hittorff worked
mostly in Paris. The extensive estate of
this famous architect and city-planner,
which included numerous travel
sketches and reconstructions of
buildings (like this one), later returned
to his native city.

3
Philipp Otto Runge
Wolgast 1777 – 1810 Hamburg
Genii on a lily, 1809
Pencil and chalk, 57 × 40.9 cm
Inv.no. 1937/9. Acquired in 1937
This is one of the many preparatory
studies for the painting *Morning* by this
important Romantic painter. The forms
emerge and take shape in finely graded
light and dark nuances.

1

2

3

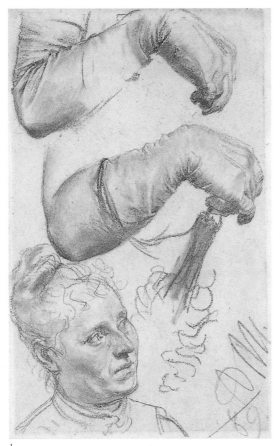

1

2

3

4

5

127

Index of artists